S0-EDH-418

JERRY J. YASUTOME
630 N. E. 106th PL.
PORTLAND, ORE. 97220

PORTLAND

A PICTORIAL HISTORY

PORTLAND

A PICTORIAL HISTORY

by Harry Stein,
Kathleen Ryan and Mark Beach

Designed by
Jamie Backus

Donning
Virginia Beach/Norfolk

Copyright© 1980 by Harry Stein, Kathleen Ryan, and Mark Beach

All rights reserved, including the right to reproduce this book in any form whatsoever without permission in writing from the publisher, except for brief passages in connection with a review. For information, write: The Donning Company/Publishers, 5041 Admiral Wright Road, Virginia Beach, Virginia 23462.

Library of Congress Cataloging in Publication Data
Portland, a pictorial history.

   1. Portland, Or.—Description—Views.
2. Portland, Or.—History—Pictorial works.
I. Stein, Harry H., 1938- II. Ryan, Kathleen, 1943- III. Beach, Mark.
F884.P843P67   979.5'49   80-20733
ISBN 0-89865-044-5 (pbk.)

Printed in the United States of America.

Portland's economy picked up as orders related to the European war began arriving in 1941. In the center distance, the decommissioned battleship Oregon is moored at the west end of the Hawthorne Bridge.
Photograph by
Alfred A. Monner

Contents

Foreword

No single book can possibly encompass the immense scope of Portland's history. These three authors, however, with the help of many cameras, have captured some significant dimensions not easily depicted in words. The authors have made the most exhaustive search ever conducted through the extensive and scattered photographic files of the city of Portland to find these images of the city's growth.

This book does more than show physical development, although the different stages of the city's expansion are well portrayed. It explains how Portland grew and why it looks the way it does today. From its earliest survey, in 1845, Portland was given the scale of a small city. The west side downtown was platted with 200-foot square blocks, bequeathing a sense of human scale that has never been totally erased by large buildings. Many Portlanders today find that small scale pleasing and comforting and wish to preserve it even at the expense of disapproving modern developments worth millions of dollars.

Although downtown receives proper consideration, the coverage reaches far beyond—north and south, and eastward across the Willamette River to neighborhood, residential and shopping districts. The Willamette itself gets primary attention because the Columbia and its famous urban tributary *made* Portland. The city's earliest fortunes were derived from river transporta-

tion. Portland's wide, deep-water port near the confluence of two navigable waterways in the very heart of a region enormously rich in natural resources preordained its early growth and prosperity. The city became the delivery end of a great funnel. Today, it ranks eleventh in the United States as a distribution center and third in ocean tonnage on the Pacific Coast.

Cities are more than simply collections of offices, factories, shopping centers, and homes. Historically, cities have been containers for diverse groups of human beings and devices for distributing a wide variety of human energies and experiences. One author wrote, "A city is a place where a small boy, as he walks through it, may see something that will tell him what he wants to do his whole life." Thus this book, without ignoring the obvious historical importance of pioneers and leading families, concentrates almost entirely on ordinary people and street scenes.

As an historical document, this book is unique for Portland, which, like most cities, has been grossly understudied, especially pictorially. Historians like myself have traditionally used photographs to illustrate text in an effort to make events or personalities more vivid. In contrast, this book uses photographs as evidence—as documents in their own right. Its 350 images capture the pulse of Portland from its early days as a river town to its modern metropolitan expanse.

E. KIMBARK MACCOLL

Preface

Portland is one of the world's few major cities whose history lies entirely within the era of photography. In addition, Portland—far from home for most newcomers and always proud of its visual wealth—has been extensively photographed. Millions of images from the past tell the city's story.

Millions of photos have little value if they are not organized and available. For three decades the Oregon Historical Society has assembled historic pictures. Its huge collection is nationally known. Equally important, the society's attention to historic images aroused interest elsewhere. Several commercial studios each have fine collections; there are dozens of industries and agencies which systematically preserve their photographs; hundreds of individuals have interests which lead them to collect old pictures. The city itself has recently established an archives which includes an important group of photos.

There are dozens of important historical facts and opinions impossible to capture on film. They will not be found in this book. While we have used words for captions and chapter introductions, we saw Portland as others had viewed it with a camera. Thus we have told only that part of the city's history which could be represented visually.

We are fond of Portland, but we also know the city has faults. Some are represented by images in this book. If the faults were not here, the city might not seem human. We tried to present Portland's history as the average person experienced it, not as it was shaped by some majestic elite or symbolized by a handful of self-important buildings.

We hope you like the city you meet in these pages and feel at home in its surroundings.

Members of the Lewis and Clark Expedition exploring the lower Willamette in 1805 named the native American residents Multnomahs. By the time Portland was settled, the Multnomahs were rarely seen in the vicinity. Late in the nineteenth century "Old John" was thought to be the last of them and perhaps to have known Lewis and Clark.
Photograph by Joseph Buchtel; from Oregon Historical Society

CHAPTER I
1843-1882

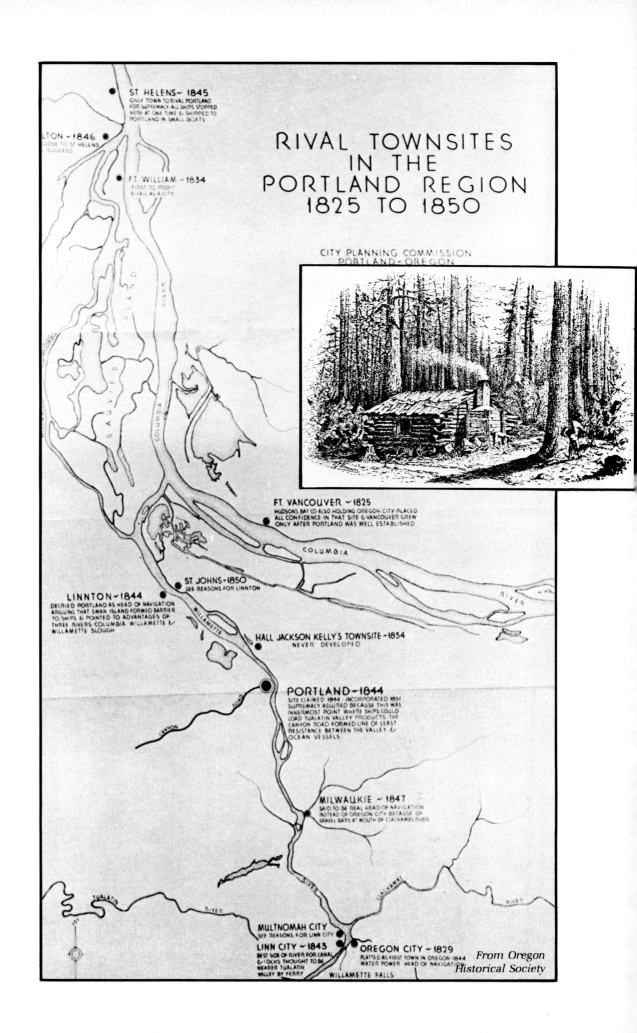

Francis Pettygrove's store was built during the winter of 1844/45 and is believed to be the first cabin within the original city limits. The site is now Front and Washington. Asa Lovejoy and William Overton made the original clearing in 1843. Pettygrove bought Overton's claim in 1844 and supposedly won a coin toss to name the area after his home town of Portland, Maine.
From Oregon Historical Society

In the summer of 1846 Navy Lieutenant Neil Howison sailed his schooner *Shark* up the Columbia River. Anchoring off the mouth of the Willamette near Fort Vancouver, he continued to Oregon City by canoe and returned overland by horseback. Howison's report included the first published description of Portland.

"Mr. F.W. Pettygrove, from Maine," wrote Lieutenant Howison, "selected Portland as the site of a town accessible to shipping, built houses, and established himself there; invited others to settle around him, and appropriated his little capital to opening wagon roads (aided by neighboring farmers) in the Twality plains. With a population of more than sixty souls, the heads of families generally industrious mechanics, its prospects of increase are favorable."

Prospects turned shortly to reality. With wagons lumbering each summer over the Oregon Trail, the settlement became a village of 500 by 1850. Portland had been discovered.

Position was as important as population. The site was at the head of navigation: as far inland as ships could go from the ocean. Farm products for export and manufactured goods for import mingled on the waterfront. Portland was already calling itself the Metropolis of the West.

Population and position favored growth, but the settlers needed persistence as well. Merely clearing the forest and building houses, stores, roads, and docks was not enough. There was keen competition from other river towns with equally grand visions of the future. To beat out Milwaukie, St. Helens, and the rest, early Portlanders ran their own steamship line to San Francisco, built a great plank road over the west hills to the farms beyond, and convinced the United States government to build a regional post office.

Portland was also lucky. The first settlers had barely staked their claims before gold was discovered in California. Thousands of miners hungered for Oregon produce and could pay in dust to keep their bellies full. When gold fever hit southern Oregon, northern Idaho and British Columbia in the 1850s and '60s, Portland was a full partner in the profits. The clearing by the river—once simply the rest stop half way between Oregon City and Vancouver—was now a trading post for the entire Northwest.

Private commerce made Portland thrive, but public buildings gave Portland pride. During the 1850s the town built its first jail, school and theater; began its first newspaper and literary society; and opened half a dozen churches. Leading citizens bragged about being second only to San Francisco in size, variety, and culture.

City parks showed civic mindedness at its best. An 1851 extension of the original town plan reserved a green strip. The land is now the Park Blocks. Again in 1871 the city bought acreage in the west hills now known as Washington Park. Both actions were exceptional for a nineteenth century American city, especially one so close to nature and the frontier as Portland.

Portland, however, never thought of itself as the frontier. Forget the wild west. People in the Oregon territory had always been orderly. Oregonians lived by the temporal law of the Hudson Bay Trading Company and the heavenly law of the Methodist missionaries. Disobedience meant going broke, being damned, or both.

When another New Englander visited Portland twenty years after its founding, he, like Lieutenant Howison before him, had nothing but praise. Samuel Bowles was a newspaper editor from Massachusetts who told his readers, "The population of Portland is about 7,000. They keep Sunday as we do in New England...and real estate is quite high—$400 a front foot for best lots 100 feet deep on the main business street. A single daily newspaper has 2,500 circulation. Altogether, Portland has the air and fact of a prosperous, energetic town with a good deal of eastern leadership and tone to business and society and morals."

In the early days successful merchants built brick buildings as status symbols. D.C. Coleman built his on Front near Oak in July 1853.

From Oregon Historical Society

Front Street in July 1852. Most of the men on the board sidewalk are employees of Wells Fargo Express Company. Henry W. Corbett (1827-1903) stands third from the right. Corbett was a hardware merchant who later became a powerful banker and, in 1866, United States Senator.

From Oregon Historical Society

Wheat and produce came to town after 1851 over the great plank road west to the Tualatin valley. The valley was Portland's main food source until World War II. This picture from the late nineteenth century shows the historic route which has become today's Canyon Road.

*From Oregon
Historical Society*

The view southwest from the corner of Front and Washington in 1854 showed solid timber at the edge of town. Portland Academy and Female Seminary, founded in 1851, stands in the woods on the corner of Jefferson and Seventh (now Broadway). The spire is on the First Congregational Church, also built in 1851, at Jefferson and Second. Bear and cougar supposedly roamed the forest beginning at Sixth Avenue.
From Oregon Historical Society

As Portlanders cut back the forest, citizens of other towns along the river dubbed their rival "Stump Town." This photo looking northeast in the late 1850s shows why. The haze over Portland is smoke from wood stoves. Stumps were whitewashed for better visibility during evening travel.
From Oregon Historical Society

Portland's volunteer fire companies join the German-language Turn Verein Association and the Jefferson Guard to celebrate the Fourth of July in 1858. The scene is on Front Street between Alder and Washington.
From Oregon Historical Society

Flooding from the Willamette was almost an annual spring event. Here eight men canoe along Front (looking north from Washington) during the high water of June 1862.
From Delano Studio/Smith

18

Women from Portland's early commercial elite pose about 1865. Many of their names— Failing, Corbett, Ogden, Bradford, and Lewis—were virtually synonymous with Portland during its early years.
From Oregon Historical Society

Employees display their tools at the wagon and carriage factory of Hay and Burch in 1865. Located on Front between today's Main and Madison streets, the factory was one of the several small manufacturing concerns serving only the local market in the pre-railway era.
From Oregon Historical Society/Oregonian

Flags hang over Front Street near Alder for the procession on April 12, 1865, to celebrate the end of the Civil War three days earlier. The telegraph message of General Lee's surrender took only one day to reach Portland via San Francisco. In contrast, accurate news of Oregon's statehood in 1859 had taken thirty-two days to come by ship during the era before telegraph, through trains, or Pony Express.

From Oregon Historical Society

The Gem Saloon, a popular oyster bar, and the Oro Fino Hall, a beer garden associated with Portland's first theater, at First and Stark about 1867.

Right from the start, culture and commerce formed a profitable partnership.

From Oregon Historical Society

The Great Western Hotel at First and Morrison, later called the Occidental Hotel, was an important center of commercial life after 1860. Stagecoach hacks wait for hotel guests under the eyes of loungers in 1869. The Webfoot Saloon on the corner shows early use of Californians' nickname for Oregonians.
From Oregon
Historical Society

Carlton Emmons Watkins, one of the great pioneer photographers of the American West, made this panorama of Portland in 1867 when the town had almost 7,000 people. The county courthouse is center left; the first state penitentiary center right.
From Oregon
Historical Society

Looking north up Front from the corner of Washington in 1872, Portland Odd Fellows march to celebrate the fifty- *third anniversary of the Odd Fellowship in the United States.*
From Oregon Historical Society

Fires in December 1872 and August 1873 destroyed thirty blocks of wooden structures in the south end of town. The photograph looking west from Front between Madison and Jefferson shows the remains in 1873 of Engine Company #4 *and the unscathed First Congregational Church. Shading on the drawing—an artist's conception—shows the burned-over area.*
Photo and map from Oregon Historical Society

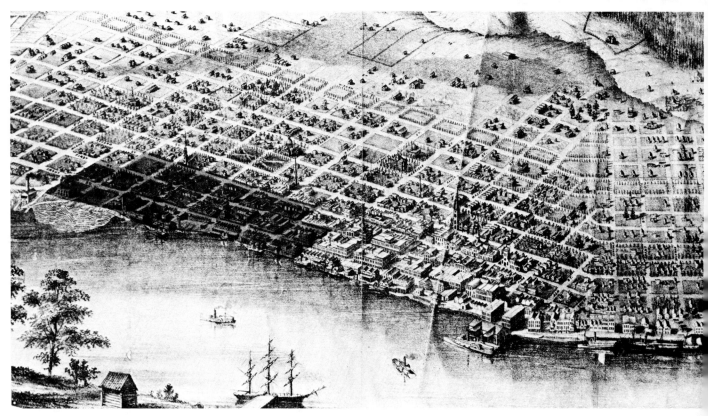

The new cast iron buildings on Front looking north from Oak withstand their first major flood in 1876.
From Delano Studio

During the 1870s steam began replacing sails in Portland harbor. Ship traffic increased dramatically.
From Oregon Historical Society

By 1880 Portland's population of 18,000 included 1,600 born in Germany.

From Oregon Historical Society

Wood was important from earliest times. Workers for Nicolai Brothers at Second and Everett show their craftsmanship in 1873.

From Oregon Historical Society

Nurses and doctors at St. Vincent's Hospital, founded in 1875 at Twelfth and Marshall, prepare to amputate the crushed leg of a porter. Lighting was crude and, before knowledge of germ theory, sterile techniques virtually unknown.

From Oregon Historical Society

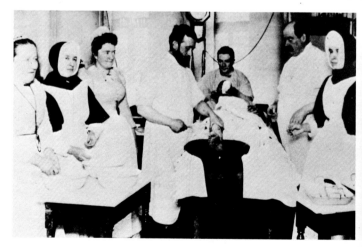

*This handful of postal employees, dressed for the mud, worked out of Oregon's first postal substation at 129 Grand Avenue in East Portland.
From Oregon Historical Society*

*Thomas Parrot's East Portland Band was considered the best of four competing at the Mechanics' Fair Pavilion in 1881. Bands such as this were often family affairs.
Photograph by I.G. Davidson; from Oregon Historical Society*

*In October 1869 the first rails were laid in East Portland for the Oregon Central Railroad Company of Salem, later part of the Southern Pacific system. The rail line, preceding East Portland's incorporation in 1870, proved a major force behind east side development.
From Oregon Historical Society*

Part of a panorama taken in 1877 by A.H. Walzen looks west along Harrison with the cupola of Harrison School in the foreground. Portland's first public school opened in 1858 with 111 pupils. By 1880, the city had four schools and 1900 pupils. Harrison and Park were the largest, each with twelve rooms and about 600 pupils.
From Oregon Historical Society

Twenty-five narrow park blocks from the West Hills to the river formed a unique part of Portland's early plans. By the time of this 1878 scene, eight blocks had been sold and built upon. Those remaining are planted with elm seedlings. The broad street to the left is North Tenth. The tower is on the top of Ladd School, now site of the Portland Art Museum.

From Oregon Historical Society

Railway trestles cross Marquam Gulch and the mainly residential South Portland area about 1881.

From Oregon Historical Society

A thinly settled East Portland lies across the Willamette in 1878. Tiny St. David's Episcopal Church appears at Grand and Sixth.

From Oregon Historical Society

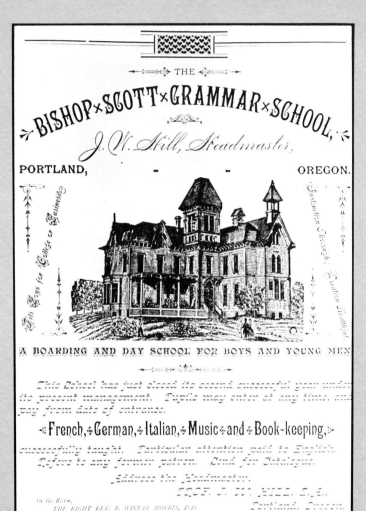

Schools and churches made a new town feel civilized. The Bishop Scott school advertised here was in a rural setting on Northwest Nineteenth between Davis and Everett.

From The West Shore, *1878*

The new post office, begun in 1869, still stands as the Pioneer Courthouse, the oldest active courthouse in the West. The west wings facing Sixth were added in 1904.

From The West Shore, *1875*

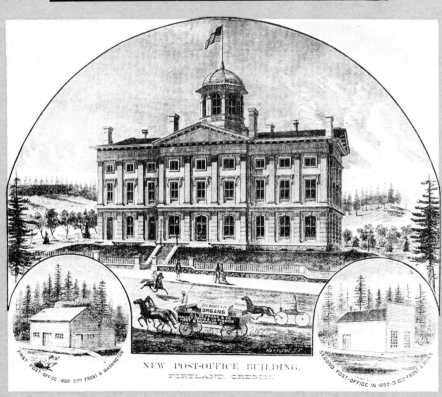

In 1874 the Temperance Women of Portland were arrested for preaching and singing in the saloons in which the city abounded—one tavern for every 250 residents. After the ladies were impounded in the new city jail at Second and Oak, this crowd gathered on the street outside.

From Oregon Historical Society

The New Market Theater on First and Ankeny was the city's pride after 1872. A produce market occupied its lower floors, theatre the upper floor from 1874 through 1885. The building still stands, but as a parking garage.

From Oregon Historical Society/Buchte' and Stotle

The Mechanics' Fair Pavilion, built in 1879 on Southwest Third between Clay and Market, provided indoor space for sports, exhibits, and concerts. These two photographs, taken in 1881, show the main pavilion floor and balcony, complete with fountain, and an exhibit of art and photography. After a new exposition building was built on Washington near Nineteenth in 1888, the original pavilion was enlarged to become the public market. The site is now occupied by the Portland Civic Auditorium.
Photographs from Oregon Historical Society

Italianate houses dominate Seventh, now Broadway, in 1880. The photograph taken from Robinson's Hill looks north. Today Interstate 405 would occupy the foreground, with Duniway Park to the immediate right down the hill.
From Oregon Historical Society

CHAPTER II
1883-1904

This idyllic conception of the mouth of the Willamette also shows Mounts St. Helens and Rainier. Views such as this were published to recruit immigrants to the Northwest.
From The West Shore, *1883*

Leo Samuel was a typical nineteenth century Portlander. Born in Germany, he had been sent as a child to live with an uncle in San Francisco. During the 1850s he learned the publishing business by selling magazines to miners.

By the 1870s Samuel was in Portland publishing a magazine called *The West Shore.* Samuel used his pen to encourage immigration to the great Northwest. "Portland," he wrote in 1883, "is now a city of 30,000 people possessing several miles of solid business blocks, having three street railway companies, enjoying the conveniences of the telephone and the advantages of the electric light, and possessing systems of gas and water works."

A fair city, indeed, and well worth attention from enterprising outsiders. Samuel was so confident of progress in Portland he even predicted "it will be but a few years before the hills are covered with handsome villas and mansions, while trade will occupy the streets as far back as Fifth."

Why not feel optimistic? After all, the heart of the city had survived the fire of 1873, the flood of 1876, and the series of national depressions following the Civil War. The rest of the city was fleshing out with mills, banks, insurance companies, and other trappings of urban life.

But if Portland a century ago was mature, it was not yet adult. The city needed transcontinental rail service to come of age. In 1883 Portland became the western terminus for Northern Pacific. The city broke out in cheers, then settled down to the pleasant task of making money from the rails.

The trains moved goods and produce, but also brought people in variety and number not seen before. It was the great age of immigration: Germans, Swedes, and Italians joined the Chinese and Irish who had previously been the town's major ethnic groups.

Rails laced the city as well as the countryside. Street cars—at first pulled by horses, then by steam, then electrified in the 1890s—allowed growth beyond easy distances by foot or horseback. Housing areas became separated from working areas, and people used new words such as "neighborhood" and "commuter."

And how the busy citizens clamored for speed! Rails on land were no longer enough—there must be rails over the river too. The first three bridges were all built within a period of six years, making downtown ferries obsolete. With the old towns of Albina and East Portland now physically joined to the city, they merged politically as well. By 1900 developers were planning neighborhoods such as Irvington and Laurelhurst on the outskirts of town.

No one captured the mood of the times better than Harvey Scott, editor of *The Oregonian* for forty years. Scott came over the Oregon Trail as a teenager in 1852, so virtually grew up with the town. Near the end of his life he remembered the coming of the railroad as "interesting, romantic, and dramatic...Like all great changes in the habits and outlook of the people, it was accompanied by an excitement of much ambition, rivalry, passion, and at length a general cloudburst of indignation and censure: but it worked its way through to a beneficent result."

This lithograph from the heyday of cast iron architecture clearly shows utility poles along Southwest Second.
     From The West Shore, *1886*

Railroad activity was concentrated on the east side throughout the 1880s. This lithograph shows Albina's railyards and shops for the Northern Pacific and Oregon and California railroads.
     From The West Shore, *1888*

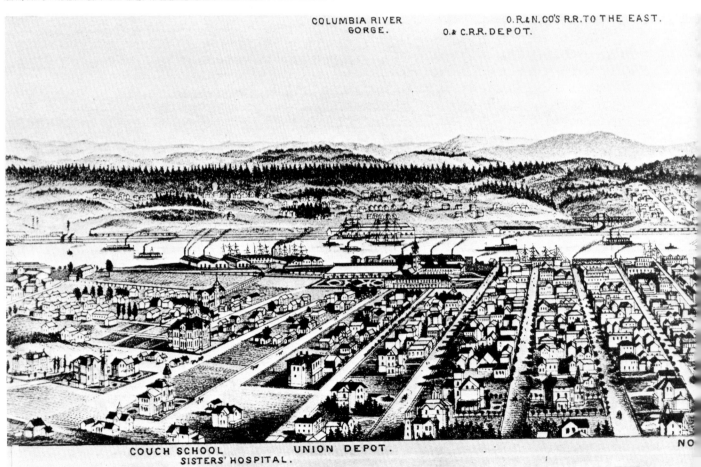

COLUMBIA RIVER   O.R.&N.CO'S R.R.TO THE EAST.
GORGE.   O.&C.R.R.DEPOT.

COUCH SCHOOL   UNION DEPOT.   NO
     SISTERS' HOSPITAL.

The whole town celebrated
when the Northern Pacific
Railroad finished its
transcontinental tie with East
Portland on September 11,
1883. Three wooden arches
were built over First Street and
a minaretted castle, also of
wood, at First and Ankeny.
  Courtesy of Frank M. Womack

Railroad magnate Henry
Villard and other Portland
boosters wanted a grand Union
Station like this.
  From The West Shore, *1882*

Portland's first illustrated
souvenir books were printed in
the 1880s and popularized
romantic panoramas such as
this.
  From Samuel's
Souvenir #1, *1883*

MT. HOOD.
11,225 FEET.
T PORTLAND SCHOOL

O. & C.R.R. TO SAN FRANCISCO.

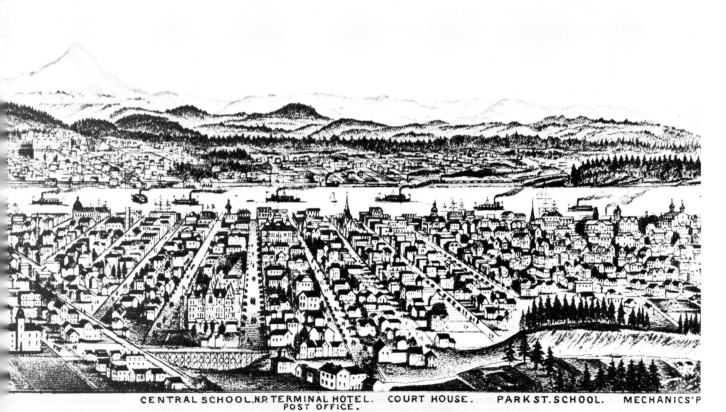

CENTRAL SCHOOL, N.P. TERMINAL HOTEL.   COURT HOUSE.   PARK ST. SCHOOL.   MECHANICS'P
POST OFFICE.

Union Station was finally built on a more practical scale in 1896.

From Oregon
Historical Society

Portland's only cable car line opened in 1890 and ran from Union Station to Portland Heights. The cars passed over the Goose Hollow trestle near Southwest Eighteenth and Jefferson.

Lithograph from The West Shore, *1890; photograph from Oregon Historical Society*

Construction of the wooden Madison Street Bridge in 1891 allowed streetcars to run from downtown to such rural locations as Mount Tabor and Milwaukie. The Madison Street Bridge was replaced by the steel Hawthorne Bridge in 1910.

From Oregon Historical Society

Streetcars had been pulled by mules through downtown as early as 1871. The cars flourished, however, in the flat east side. This 1888 scene is the corner of Grand and East Morrison.

From Oregon Historical Society/Bates

Metropolitan St. Johns in the 1880s, when sailing ships were powered down the river by steam.

From Oregon Historical Society/Miner

The Portland Flour Mills and Pacific Coast Elevator made Albina in the 1890s a major Northwest milling center.

From The West Shore, 1890

In 1886 the United States Fish Commission shipped 600,000 shad eggs from Maryland to Portland in this railroad car. Agents stocked the surviving fry into the Willamette River, opening a new era in sport and commercial fishing.
Courtesy of United States National Archives

Albina was heavily settled by Irish immigrants in the 1880s. By the 1890s it was an international polyglot, including Swedes, Norwegians, Germans, Finns, Estonians, Latvians, and Poles. By 1900 East European immigrants also were flowing heavily into St. Johns, Linnton, and South Portland.
Courtesy of Portland Parks and Recreation Bureau

Boarding houses furnished inexpensive housing for both single people and families. This boarding house of Abramo and Ciuseppiria Cereghino at 236 Front Street was popular with Italian immigrants in the 1890s. The pine tree in front helped newcomers identify the building.

From Oregon Historical Society

The Right Reverend B. Wistar Morris, far right, founded Good Samaritan Hospital and Orphanage in 1875, and for thirty-eight years was Episcopal Bishop for Oregon. Here he and friends display their catch taken after church services sometime in the 1890s.
Courtesy of Good Samaritan Hospital and Medical Center

Before the University of Oregon medical school was built, Marquam Hill was an area of simple houses with fenced yards and gardens.
From Oregon Historical Society

Picnicking on Ross Island.
From The West Shore, *1886*

The Couch family, a powerful
and closeknit pioneer clan,
picnic in City Park (now
Washington Park) in 1889.
                    From Oregon
              Historical Society

Informal lunch at the Walter J. Burns' cottage above Willamette Heights in 1894. Mrs. Burns was a grandaughter of Captain John Couch, whose decision to locate his shipping in Portland launched the area as an international port.

From Oregon Historical Society

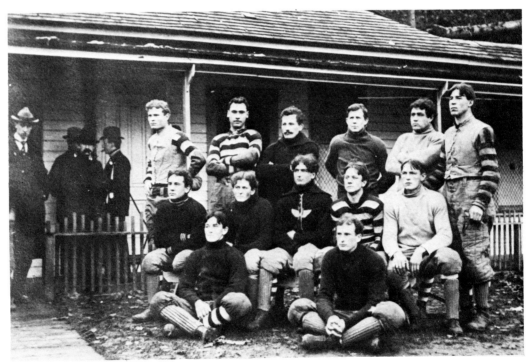

Late nineteenth century sports largely meant vigorous amateurs using minimal equipment before small crowds. The Multnomah Amateur Athletics Club, founded in 1891, fielded this football team in 1898.

From Oregon Historical Society

45

MAN'S LIFE IS FULL OF TROUBLE AND TEMPTATION. HE COMES INTO THIS WORLD WITHOUT HIS CONSENT AND GOES OUT OF IT AGAINST HIS WILL. HIS JOURNEY THROUGH LIFE IS ROCKY AND BESET WITH STRANGE AND CONTRADIC-TORY EXPERIENCES. WHEN HE IS LITTLE THE BIG GIRLS KISS HIM, AND WHEN HE IS BIG THE LITTLE GIRLS KISS HIM. WHEN HE IS A BOY HE WISHES HE WERE A MAN, AND WHEN HE IS A MAN HE WISHES HE WERE A BOY AGAIN. IF HE RAISED A LARGE FAMILY HE IS A CHUMP. IF HE RAISES A CHECK, HE IS A THIEF. IF HE IS POOR, HE IS A BAD MANAGER, AND IF HE IS RICH, HE IS DISHONEST. IF HE IS IN POLITICS, IT IS FOR GRAFT, AND IF HE IS OUT OF POLITICS YOU CAN'T PLACE HIM, AND HE IS NO GOOD TO HIS COUNTRY.

IF HE GIVES TO CHARITY, IT IS FOR SHOW, AND IF HE DOES NOT GIVE HE IS A STINGY CUSS. IF HE DIES YOUNG, THERE WAS A GREAT FUTURE BEFORE HIM, AND IF HE LIVES TO AN OLD AGE HE MISSED HIS CALLING. IF HE IS ACTIVE IN RELIG-ION, HE IS A HYPOCRITE, AND IF HE TAKES NO INTEREST IN RELIGIOUS MAT-TERS HE IS A HARDENED SINNER. IF HE SHOWS AFFECTION, HE IS A SOFT SPECI-MEN, AND IF HE SHOWS NONE HE IS A COLD PROPOSITION.

IN ORDER TO ENJOY LIFE PROPERLY AND TO BE ALWAYS HEALTHY HE MUST EAT, SMOKE WHEN HE WANTS TO, SEE THAT THE AIR IS PROPERLY STERILIZED BEFORE BREATHING AND DRINK "RHEIN-GOLD."

THE NEW DRAUGHT BEER FOR SALE AT THE BARS OF THE HEADQUARTER'S SA-LOON, 285 ALDER STREET, HOF BRAU, OREGON GRILLE, QUELLE.

THE HENRY WEINHARD BREWERY,

A-1172.   13TH AND BURNSIDE.   MAIN 72.

The Weinhard Brewery dates from 1856 and sold its products mainly through its own saloons during the nineteenth century. Company advertisements have always linked the good life in Oregon with the local brew.

Photo courtesy of Jewish Historical Society of Oregon; advertisement from Oregon Historical Society

The short-lived Cordray's theatre in 1890 was as important as the Marquam Grand in presenting big names from the concert and theatre worlds.

*From Oregon
Historical Society*

Amateur as well as professional thespians have long trod Portland's boards. At the Marquam Grand theatre, opened in 1890 at Sixth and Alder, the Multnomah Athletic Club performed Mr. and Mrs. Cleopatra around the turn of the century.

*From Oregon
Historical Society*

August Erickson's saloon on Second and Burnside from the 1890s to the 1920s boasted the longest bar in the world, a skylit ballroom and stage, stained glass, and real grapes growing along the balcony. Loggers, sailors, cattlemen, and townsfolk also patronized the brothel in small, closed cribs around the balcony. From such waterfront saloons the unwary were sometimes shanghaied for ship crews.

Courtesy of Erickson's Cafe and Concert Hall

Elizabeth Barchus became famous as The Oregon Artist for her thousands of paintings of Mount Hood. Widowed with young children, she established a successful studio in the old Multnomah block on Morrison Street.

From Oregon Historical Society/Oregon Journal

Checkout desk of the private membership library at Southwest Stark between Broadway and Park in the 1890s. The Library Association of Portland opened its doors to the public in 1902 and arranged, partly with public funds, to open the current building on Southwest Tenth in 1913.

From Oregon Historical Society/Oregon Journal

Portland's first bridge across the Willamette opened in April 1887. The artist for this lithograph of the Morrison Street Bridge stood on the east bank looking west to be sure downtown clearly showed.

From The West Shore, 1887

The riverboat fleet of the Shaver Transportation Company at the foot of Washington Street in 1897. Generations of Portlanders could identify individual boats by the distinctive sounds of their whistles.

From Oregon Historical Society/Shaver Transportation

Small shipyards up and down the Willamette built wooden cargo schooners for river and ocean trade. These men, in silk hats probably as a joke, caulked decks with irons and mallets.

From Oregon Historical Society

Ferries plied the river until gradually replaced by bridges. Here the Sellwood ferry crosses from the west side at the site of the current bridge. Ferry service continued to Sellwood until the bridge was built in the 1920s.

Courtesy of Portland Parks and Recreation Bureau

The worst flood of Portland's first 100 years covered 250 blocks on both sides of the Willamette in June 1894. The water rose slowly, inundating homes, shops, and businesses. Sidewalks and merchandise were elevated to second and sometimes third floors and, with 1,500 boats pressed into temporary service, business proceeded somewhat as usual. The fire department moved pumpers on barges like the one shown here at Second and Washington in Chinatown. Inside the Chamber of Commerce building on Stark between Third and Fourth, people posed for the numerous photographers recording the flood for wonder and profit.

Photographs from Oregon Historical Society

*Portland's harbor in 1899.
Photograph by H.A. Hale; from
Oregon Historical Society*

*The Alaska gold rush in the
spring of 1897 set off a minor
economic boom. This shipment
for April 7, 1898, was
assembled at 20 North Front
Street.*

*From Oregon
Historical Society*

The 1891 Fourth of July parade route included First Avenue.
From Oregon Historical Society

Portlanders first climbed Mount Hood in 1857. The Alpine Club was organized in 1887 and another group, the Mazamas, in 1894. Here a lighthearted group sets out for the mountain on July 7, 1896.
From Oregon Historical Society

East Portland in 1898 looking east toward Mount Tabor and Mount Hood. The Madison Street (now Hawthorne Street) Bridge, built in 1891, shows at the far right.
Photograph by H. A. Hale; from Oregon Historical Society

When climbers reached snow level they blackened their faces as protection against the sun.

From Oregon
Historical Society

During the 1890s Portland shared in the national bicycling craze. Bike paths were built everywhere (many becoming automobile routes after the turn of the century). One popular route led north from town to the Vancouver ferry. Local farmers would sell fruit and lemonade along the way, and on a warm Sunday the ferry might take 3,000 riders round trip across the Columbia. The Mount Tabor Reservoir, shown here, was also a favorite destination in the countryside.

From Oregon Historical Society

This playground on the North Park Blocks around 1900 served affluent northwest Portlanders. The city's park system was expanded dramatically in the 1920s to serve the dozens of new neighborhoods.
Photograph by Benjamin Gifford; from Oregon Historical Society

Captain Nathaniel Crosby's house was shipped in sections from New England and built as the first frame building in Portland in 1847. Here on Northwest Fourth about 1900 it housed a vegetarian restaurant and offices for the Oregon Native Son, a monthly magazine..

From Oregon Historical Society

Members of the Journeyman Bakers and Confectioners Union #114 pose on Park Street with other American Federation of Labor locals and their floats in the 1902 Labor Day parade. Portland was largely a non-union town.

From Oregon Historical Society

The Portland Board of Trade poses in front of its blackboards long before computers kept track of market quotations. The board evolved into the new Chamber of Commerce in 1890.

From Oregon Historical Society

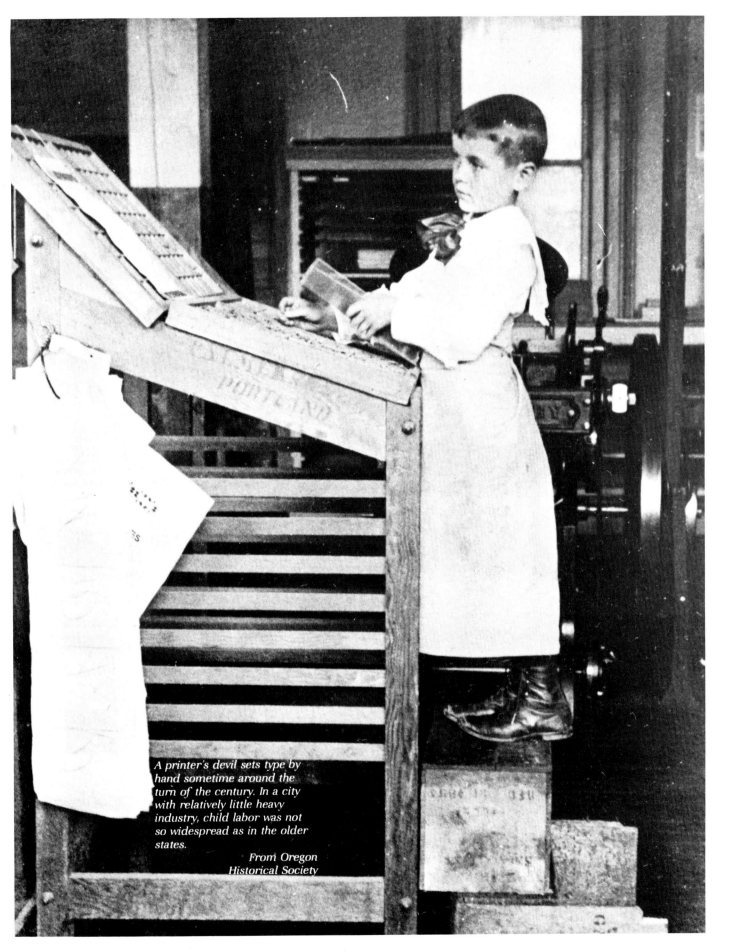

A printer's devil sets type by hand sometime around the turn of the century. In a city with relatively little heavy industry, child labor was not so widespread as in the older states.

From Oregon Historical Society

By the turn of the century the old one-story frame houses were being replaced downtown by multi-story buildings of stone, iron, or steel. This scene is at the northeast corner of Third and Salmon. Meanwhile many neighborhoods, such as Sabin, still had gravel roads and wooden sidewalks.
From Oregon Historical Society

Portland's small but influential German Jewish community favored Temple Beth Israel. This wooden building burned in 1923 and was replaced by the present structure at the corner of Northwest Nineteenth and Flanders.
From The West Shore, *1888*

This turn-of-the-century funeral procession entered Lone Fir Cemetery at Southeast Morrison and Twentieth.
From Oregon Historical Society

Looking east over Goose Hollow in 1900. The grocery at the lower right is now the corner of Southwest Seventeenth and Market. The building with two spires at the upper left is Temple Beth Israel. The First Congregational Church tower stands in the middle, while the Calvary Presbyterian Church, now known as The Old Church, stands at the right.
Photograph by J.P. Ford; from Oregon Historical Society

Mayor David Thompson presented the Elk Fountain to Portland in 1900. Placed between the two courthouse squares, now the Plaza blocks, it acted as a gateway for center downtown. Humans and beasts alike found its water refreshing. Despite the growing tawdriness of the squares and the fountain's later danger to auto drivers, it remained Portland's best-known symbol.
Courtesy of John (Woody) Conley

CHAPTER III
1905-1919

*Downtown Portland in 1912
taken from King's Heights
looking east toward Mount
Hood.*

*Photograph by George
Weister; from Vintage
Photos/Elaine Gobel*

At the turn of the century Portland had 90,000 citizens: from clearing to village to town to city, all in sixty years. Downtown bustled with people, horses, wagons, carriages, trolleycars, and trains. Dust and smells were often stifling, noise usually intense. Iron wheels and horseshoes rattled constantly against rails and cobblestones.

As fast as Portland grew, it never boomed. Its healthy economy had roots in diversity rather than speculation. As a center of agriculture, it shipped to the world. As a center of commerce, it was still trading post for the Northwest. And as a center of manufacturing, it was growing strong. There were logs to cut, ships to build and heavy machines to make. Finally, money flowed as blocks filled with houses, stores, factories, and office buildings.

Yet all that was not enough. Business interests, especially real estate developers, wanted faster growth. The surge of people and cash brought by the railroad was twenty years old and fading. More important, upstart towns such as Tacoma and Seattle had their own railroads. Seattle was the staging grounds for the Alaska gold rush. Its boosters were bragging about growing bigger than Portland.

Something had to be done, and that something was the Lewis and Clark Exposition of 1905. Almost overnight a fairyland showcase sprang up around Guild's Lake. Portland displayed itself as a hardworking city of homes, churches, and flowers. Thousands of electric globes lit the midway; dozens of states and nations sent exhibits.

The event worked exactly as planned. Three million people came to the party. Thousands decided to stay—so many thousands that Portland's population doubled within five years. Indeed, during the next decade the city became so big it swallowed up the neighboring towns of Lents, Montavilla, St. Johns, and Linnton.

More people meant more of everything required by city life. A score of new grade schools dotted the neighborhoods. Three new high schools opened the doors to higher education. When Reed College opened in 1912, temporary streetcar tracks carried proud citizens across the campus directly to the speaker's platform. A second major newspaper—*The Oregon Journal*—was as welcome as the new movie theaters.

And the party continued. The same streetcars which brought workers downtown and to the factories on weekdays served the opposite ends of the lines on weekends. Oaks Park, Council Crest, Hayden Island, and half a dozen courses for the fashionable game of golf became popular destinations. The Pacific International Livestock Exposition grew into an annual event. To top it all off, a group of boosters in 1907 began the first annual parade featuring floats decorated with roses.

The town was not, of course, all fun and beauty. Gambling, booze, and brothels had their share of the profits and perhaps a bit more. Worse yet—and harder to see—Portland was turning its back on the river. Signs had been there as early as 1890 when Willamette water was no longer potable and miles of rails lined each shore. During the next decade, engineers had laid thirty miles of pipe to bring pure water from Bull Run to the new reservoirs on Mt. Tabor and in Washington Park.

Finally, of course, there was the automobile. During the exposition it had been merely a cantankerous toy. In 1910 Meier and Frank switched from horses to engines to pull delivery trucks. Even outlying farmers were converting from oats to gasoline. By 1919 no house without a garage could be considered truly fashionable.

Logs are hoisted into place for the "largest log cabin in the world"—the Forestry Building to celebrate the wood products industry.
Courtesy of Portland Parks and Recreation Bureau

The Forestry Building proved one of the Exposition's most popular attractions. Built in the woods near the current Montgomery Ward store, the building was a landmark until it burned in 1964.
From Oregon Historical Society

The Lewis and Clark Exposition of 1905 included a sunken garden, arcaded bridge, and carnival midway. There were statues built of plaster of paris, terraces, and flowers everywhere. Here, looking north across Guild's Lake, lights outline the Government Building and causeway.

From Oregon Historical Society

Lincoln Beachey's airship, first flown at the St. Louis Fair in 1904, rises from near the Government Building over the lake for the first successful lighter-than-air flight on the Pacific Coast.

From Oregon Historical Society/Blossom

Visitors descend the grand staircase. The Exposition site near the west bank of the river across from Swan Island is now known as the Northwest Industrial District.

From Oregon Historical Society

The Willamette Iron and Steel Works, dating from 1865, is one of Portland's oldest and best-known industries. It made ships and ship machinery, industrial boilers and logging machines. This yarder, the type that mechanized logging, is built onto a flatcar. When located in the woods, the apparatus hauled logs directly to the railhead.

From Oregon Historical Society/WISCO

Employee lunchrooms, particularly with table service, were still rare in the 1910s when these workers at Willamette Iron and Steel glanced up for the photographer.

From Oregon Historical Society/WISCO

Portland boosters were thrilled by the grand era of city beautiful visions which swept the nation. The 1909 sketch of New York on the Willamette was fanciful, but the 1912 Bennett plan perfectly serious. The plan called for massive buildings along West Burnside and the North Park Blocks, all leading to a new Union Station.

Drawings from Oregon Historical Society

The German bark Lisbeth loads directly at the Eastern and Western mill in the Slabtown area. Portland's prospering world trade was only temporarily interrupted when Europe went to war in 1914.

Photograph by Harold M Brown; courtesy of Frank M Womack

64

Looking north in 1910 toward
Mount Saint Helens and,
further north and west,
Mounts Ranier and Baker!
Balfour-Guthrie Company's 800
foot Oceanic Dock in Albina
burned in 1914.
Photograph by George Weister;
from Vintage Photos/Elaine
Gobel

Photograph by Kathleen Ryan

Visitors board the battleship Oregon, flagship of the Pacific fleet, in Portland harbor about 1916. The Oregon was commissioned in 1896, saw extensive action in the Spanish-American War, and was scrapped in 1943. Her mast, however, still stands sentinel in Waterfront Park.

From Oregon Historical Society

Rail cars unload for the Supple-Ballin shipyards, East Oak at Water, about 1918.
Photograph by Benjamin Gifford; from Oregon Historical Society

A wooden hull inside the shed of Grant Smith-Porter Company, foot of Baltimore in St. Johns, in 1918. Photographers during 1918 recorded every step of ship-building and launching at Portland's expanded wartime shipyards. Companies built several hulls at once, often beneath great sheds such as this. The demands of ship-building also boosted Portland's machine shops and rail facilities.
Photograph by Benjamin Gifford; from Oregon Historical Society

Decking begins on the Elvira Stolt, *then known simply as Hull #9, at the Columbia* Engineering Works in Linnton. *From Oregon Historical Society*

The Peninsula Shipbuilding Company launches the S.S. Braxton *into the Columbia River in 1918. The United States Shipping Board, a Federal agency, ordered most of the wartime vessels.*
From Oregon Historical Society

The Chiquimula *after completion in February 1918 at the Columbia Engineering Works in Linnton.*

From Oregon Historical Society

Teamsters pose for their portrait on the Nickum and Kelly wharf at the foot of Southeast Alder in 1905. In a few years the men would be driving trucks. The dredge was vital to the river-based economy.

From Oregon Historical Society

At the turn of the century Scowtown was a hodgepodge of some 150 floating shanties on the east shore of the Willamette, concentrated between the Burnside and Madison Bridges. Residents worked nearby as fishermen, tug hands, dock and sawmill workers. Floating saloons and brothels sometimes moored beside homes of proper families. Land dwellers, however, looked upon them all as squatters paying neither rent nor taxes.

From Oregon Historical Society

In an age when the farm was still close to the collective psyche, pets came in all forms. Photograph by A.L. Campbell; courtesy of Portland Audubon Society

Ferries still carried cattle on their way to slaughter. By 1910 the boats also carried trucks such as this one from Weeks Transfer.

From Oregon Historical Society

Beginning in the 1890s, developers laid out new neighborhoods, built houses, and sold real estate. Most developments, such as Irvington in the Northeast, followed the standard gridiron plan. Some, however, such as the 126-acre Ladd's Addition in the Southeast, shown here, sought more congenial designs.

From Oregon Historical Society

Chinese street vendors sold vegetables from shoulder baskets. Many gardened near their homes at the south end of Multnomah Athletic Field prior to the 1909 expansion of the Multnomah Athletic Club.

From Oregon Historical Society/Photo-Art

As living areas became more separate from working areas, neighborhoods grew into status symbols. Some, such as Laurelhurst, even required buyers to sign deeds designed to keep out Blacks and Orientals.

From Oregon Historical Society

Most contractors worked from a standard set of blueprints which allowed only slight variations in roof design or window placement. Here workers pose in front of a typical house in Irvington about 1910.

From Oregon Historical Society

Within ten minutes of the business district at the **head** of Washington Street.

Kings & Arlington Heights
The Most Beautiful Residence Section of Portland

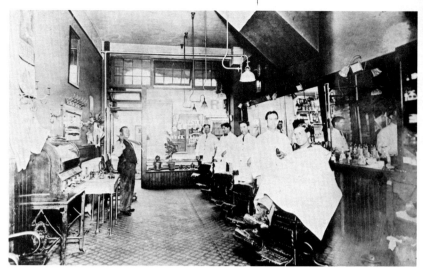

Sellwood was planned in 1882 by real estate developers as a working class suburban town. For years its population was highly transient. Ed Trites, pictured here in 1913, opened its first barber shop on Thirteenth Avenue between Umatilla and Horney.
Courtesy of Portland Parks and Recreation Bureau

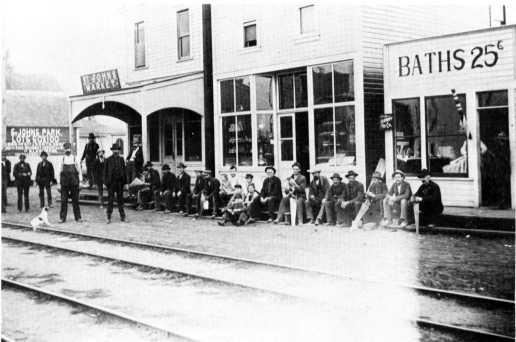

St. Johns at the time of the Lewis and Clark Exposition was a sleepy river town of about 500 souls—the size of Portland in 1850. The area boomed when thousands of Exposition visitors returned to work at the Portland Woolen Mills, established in 1904 on North Baltimore. Within ten years the town had 5,000 people and had voted to become part of Portland, mainly for access to pure water. Jersey Street in this 1906 photo is today's North Lombard.
From Oregon Historical Society

In 1919 Elmer Anderson displays the flag at his meat store at 819 Mississippi Avenue. The intense patriotism of World War I often carried over after the war in the form of hostility toward immigrants, minorities, and suspected "radicals." In the early 1920s the hostility was symbolized by Ku Klux Klan activity.
From Oregon Historical Society

Small, family-owned stores close to residences dotted Portland neighborhoods. George Skoog had this grocery at 631 Mississippi about 1917.   *From Oregon Historical Society*

Figures molded in butter, lard or ice graced table displays in fine restaurants and at formal dinners. A 215-pound butter cow had udderly fascinated strollers on the Lewis and Clark Midway. The Hazelwood Creamery, Front and Ankeny Streets, won a state fair competition in 1915 with this 261-pound duo.

From Oregon Historical Society

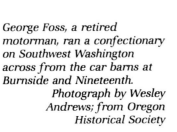

George Foss, a retired motorman, ran a confectionary on Southwest Washington across from the car barns at Burnside and Nineteenth.
Photograph by Wesley Andrews; from Oregon Historical Society

In 1870 Portland's population was twenty-five percent Chinese, in 1880 fifty percent. By 1890 Portland's Chinatown was second only to San Francisco's. Most Chinese were single males recruited to America to build railroads and operate fisheries. Many ended up as household servants. Chinese funerals such as this one in 1905 were a popular curiosity for the rest of the city.

From Oregon Historical Society/Oregonian

Japanese men, more often accompanied by wives and families than the Chinese, came to work in canneries and mills around the turn of the century. Here adults about 1906 mourn a child at the Dunning, McEnteen and Gilbaugh Funeral Home on Southeast Alder.

From Oregon Historical Society/Century

Henry Wemme brought a Stanley Steamer to Portland in November 1899 and initiated the auto age. During the transition years, animals and cars lived side by side. Here they share water at the Mount Tabor Reservoir gatehouse at Sixtieth and Southeast Division.

Courtesy of Bureau of Water Works, City of Portland

The facade of a livery stable about 1910 also made a good billboard. Women with regard for their reputations avoided saloons except for the family-style German beer gardens.

From Oregon Historical Society

Powerful horses pulling heavy wagons were a common sight for decades. In about 1906 Cornelius Makelaar drove this wagon for the Albina Fuel Company.

*From Oregon Historical Society/*Oregon Journal

Generations of Portlanders bought slabwood from mills and seasoned it next to the street before having it cut for basement storage. Itinerant sawyers cut slabs into heating lengths while neighborhood children hustled deliveries. Oldtimers still recall the sweet aroma of fresh-cut fir filling homes as winter approached.

Courtesy of John (Woody) Conley

Portland softened the impact of its great ice storms with the name Silver Thaw. This Thaw on January 6, 1912, devastated the wires near Southeast Alder and Seventeenth.

From Oregon Historical Society

Students play outside Ladd School, once one of the two largest grade schools and now the site for the Portland Art Museum at Southwest Park and Madison.
Photograph by Benjamin Gifford; from Oregon Historical Society

Portland's passion for gardens included the school system. Here students tend the garden of Ainsworth School, Southwest Vista and Twenty-First.

From Oregon Historical Society

The Holladay School store reflects the school's interracial neighborhood about 1918. The school was at Northeast Sixth and Clackamas, until recently site for the school district headquarters. Railroad employment attracted Portland's first small Black settlement in the 1880s. The only other work available was as domestics, janitors, porters, or waiters.

Photograph by Benjamin Gifford; from Oregon Historical Society

Public school children tour the Portland Art Museum, which opened in 1905.
Photograph by Benjamin Gifford; from Oregon Historical Society

A coeducational home economics class at Shattuck School, now part of Portland State University campus.
Photograph by Benjamin Gifford; from Oregon Historical Society

Graduates of an unidentified high school sit for the camera in 1904.
Courtesy of Portland Public Schools

Neighborhood House, which sponsored this sewing circle about 1912, was the first unified organization to help immigrants. The settlement house was one of 800 organizations identified within Portland's small Jewish community between 1893 and 1950.
Courtesy of Jewish Historical Society of Oregon

The children's ward of Good Samaritan Hospital about 1910 was noted for kindness and coziness. Hospitals and medical education were expanding in Portland as population grew and leaders became more aware of public health needs.
Courtesy of Good Samaritan Hospital and Medical Center

Early in this century the gospel wagon from the Apostolic Faith Church toured the North Park Blocks each Sunday.
Courtesy of Apostolic Faith Church

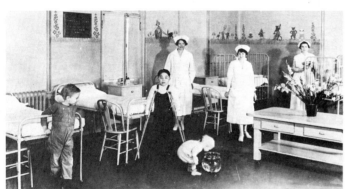

Simeon Reed made his fortune in lumber and left it to education. When his friend and business associate William Ladd donated the land, Reed College was formally founded in 1909. Although classes on the 100-acre campus began in 1912, the college continued to draw thousands to its eight extension centers. This 1916 audience is in Turn Verein Hall between Main and Jefferson on Thirteenth.

Courtesy of Reed College

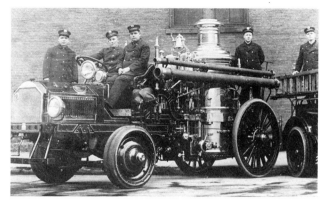

*Engine Company #3 as it
appeared shortly after
motorized fire trucks first
came to Portland in 1913.*
*From Oregon
Historical Society*

*For generations Portlanders
thrilled to racing horses
pulling fire engines. Citizens
also visited firehouses to feed
and pet animals such as Tom,
Mack, and Dad emerging here
from Engine Company #2.
Horses were finally replaced
in 1925 by trucks. This building
still stands on the corner of
Northwest Third and Glisan.*
*From Oregon Historical
Society/Oregon Journal*

*Fire pumpers fight the
devastating Union Oil Company
fire on East Water near the
Morrison Bridge on June 26,
1911. Popular fire chief David
Campbell died in the fire. The
city installed a plaque in his
honor at West Burnside on
Nineteenth and named a
fireboat for him. Oil storage
was soon moved outside the
city center.*
*From Oregon
Historical Society*

83

*Vehicles of all sorts made
daily runs to Union Station
early in the 1900s.*
*Courtesy of John
(Woody) Conley*

*In 1905 Fifth and Morrison was
the center of Portland's
business district. Then as now,
the Meier and Frank
Department Store was across
from the Pioneer Courthouse.
The Portland Hotel peeks out*
*of the rain from Sixth Avenue.
Wires over the streets carried
power to the streetcar via the
trolley; note the raised pole
and wheel touching the wire.*
*From Oregon
Historical Society*

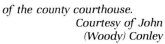

*About 1910 the Southern
Pacific Railroad ran south
along Fourth Avenue in front*
of the county courthouse.
*Courtesy of John
(Woody) Conley*

Seventh Avenue (now Broadway) will be washed by the horse-drawn sprinkler. Jackson Tower, recently completed in 1912, and the Portland Hotel stand on the east side of the street.

Courtesy of John (Woody) Conley

Portlanders loved civic decoration on an elaborate scale. The parade route for the National Elks Convention in 1912 featured stuffed elks extended from upper floor windows along Seventh (later Broadway) and a flag-bedecked Washington lined with ceremonial posts and arches. Sixteen thousand conventioneers

formed a parade seventy-five blocks long. Convention business was conducted in the armory on Northwest Tenth, which, even then, was surrounded by the brewery.
Photograph by George Weister; from Vintage Photos/Elaine Gobel Courtesy of John (Woody) Conley

Third Avenue merchants in June 1914 financed the Great Light Way of arches similar to the earlier wooden and plaster structures used for civic decoration. Sometimes illuminated, the arches remained in place until the late 1930s.

From Oregon Historical Society

The front courtyard of the Portland Hotel faced the Pioneer Courthouse on Southwest Sixth between Morrison and Yamhill. At the turn of the century, the courtyard often became a stage for performances by small groups.

From Oregon Historical Society

The Helig Theatre, Broadway and Yamhill, would bring out chairs and benches for its waiting matinee crowd. This line in 1912 stretches down Broadway past the old First Unitarian Church.

From Oregon Historical Society/Angelus

The Portland, a seven-storied Queen Anne chateau finished in 1890, was for sixty years the city's most prestigious hotel. Razed in 1951, the site became the parking garage across Sixth from the Pioneer Courthouse.

From Oregon Historical Society

Early in the century a Chinese cobbler ran this shoe repair shop from the sidewalk near the corner of Second and Alder. The Chinese community was centered along Second for several blocks south of Burnside.
From Oregon Historical Society/Oregonian

Portland police officers lead the grand parade on Broadway to open the 1910 baseball season. The Lyric Theatre is across from the Pacific Gas and Electric Building and the Bijou Nickelodeon.
From Oregon Historical Society

In 1902 George L. Baker created the Baker Stock Company, a popular repertory theatre and sometime vaudeville house.
From Oregon Historical Society

The J.K. Gill Company was founded in 1870 and grew with the national trend toward office work beginning in the 1890s. Here a salesman in 1916 displays the very latest in efficient equipment.
Courtesy of J.K. Gill Company

The Carroll Public Market on Southwest Yamhill between Third and Fifth thrived from 1914 into the 1920s. In the 1930s, it was replaced by the Public Market Building on the waterfront.
From Oregon Historical Society/Ashford

During the First World War food production and processing along with shipbuilding, fisheries, and the lumber industry were all booming statewide and feeding Portland's economy. Here women process fruit and vegetables for Lange and Company Wholesalers at First and Ankeny.
From Oregon Historical Society

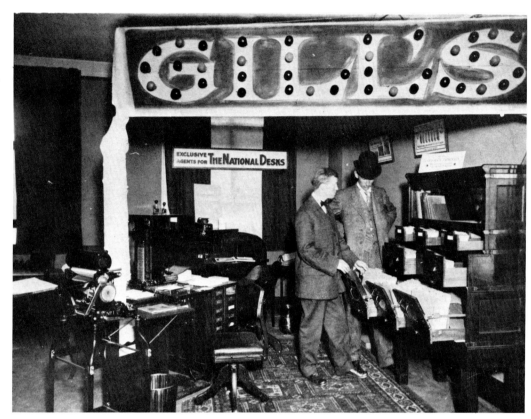

As a stunt, an open biplane piloted by Silas Cristofferson successfully takes off from a ramp especially built atop the Multnomah Hotel on June 11, 1912. The newly opened hotel facing Pine between Third and Fourth was Portland's largest. Federal government offices now occupy the building.

From Oregon Historical Society

This beach on the Columbia River was near the present site of the Interstate Bridge. Local residents had for years used the spot for swimming and picnicking. Its popularity grew in 1916 when the Portland Railway Light and Power Company connected it to the streetcar system.

From Oregon Historical Society/Columbia

Everyone knew about the marvelous flying machines, but few could actually take a ride. Anyone, however, could be photographed touring Portland in the cutout found at most amusement parks.

From Oregon Historical Society

In 1907 investors developed Council Crest as an amusement park. The park and its observatory were popular stopoffs for sightseeing excursions taken by streetcar. Closed as a private amusement park in 1929, the area became a city park in 1937. The last streetcar ran to Council Crest in 1951.

Photograph by Wesley Andrews; from Oregon Historical Society

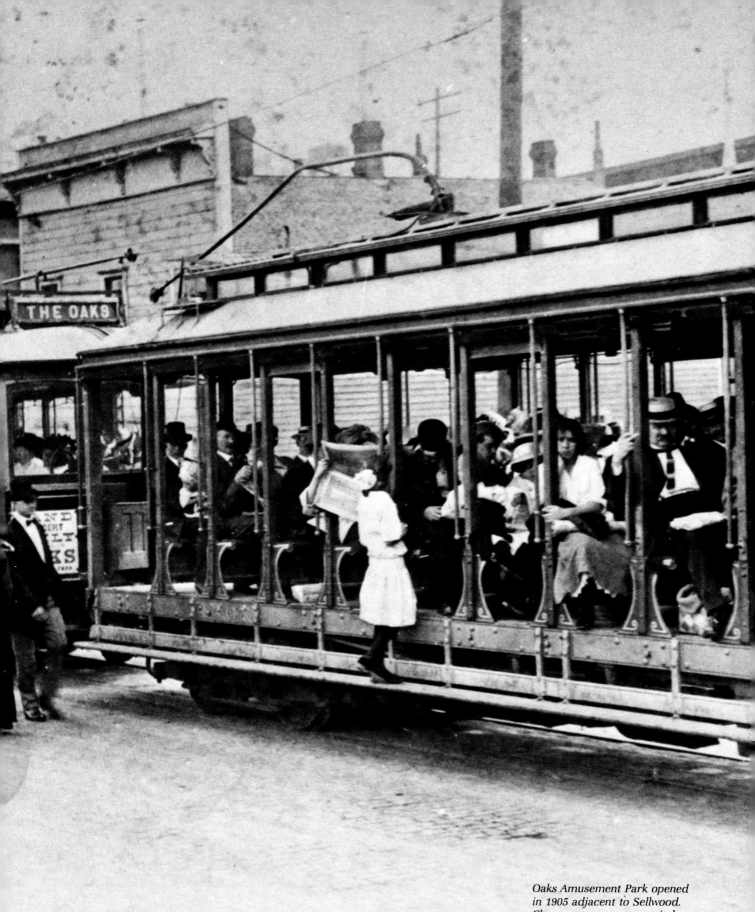

Oaks Amusement Park opened
in 1905 adjacent to Sellwood.
Cheap, easy access was vital.
Here people board open cars
of the Interurban Electric,
bound for a day at the Oaks.
From Oregon
Historical Society

Concerts, vaudeville, rides, rollerskating, dancing, and food: there was something for everyone at Oaks Park.
From Oregon Historical Society

Open buses such as these carried visitors to the Lewis and Clark Exposition and on other outings.
From Oregon Historical Society

*Supervising the streetcar line
required men of stature.
From Oregon
Historical Society*

A prize float from 1919 featured women in swim suits made by the new Jantzen Company.

Courtesy of Jantzen Incorporated

Portland's Rose Festival developed in 1907 from the city's love of roses and the earlier activities of the Portland Rose Society, founded in 1889. The festival has been held each June since, with the exception of 1918 and 1926. These warriors decorated the first prize float in the first Rose Festival Parade.

From Oregon Historical Society

Most early Rose Parade floats were mounted on flatcars and hauled by horses over the streetcar tracks. Even in the early days, however, there was a drive to be different as shown in this image from the 1912 Parade.

From Oregon Historical Society

The Portland Railway Light and Power Company delighted the 1915 Rose Parade audience with this portable display of electric illumination. Then as now, Chinook salmon were a favorite Oregon theme.

From Oregon Historical Society

THE FOOD OF KINGS AND THE KING OF FOODS

Volunteers on Sunday, March 10, 1918, built Liberty Temple between Pioneer Courthouse and the Portland Hotel to kick off a drive for war bonds. The temple served ten months as headquarters for service personnel and the Government Employment Service.

From Oregon Historical Society

97

*Thousands gathered on Valentine's Day 1917 to dedicate the
Interstate Bridge. The span connecting Portland with Vancouver
carried both autos and streetcars. Because Oregon voters had
approved prohibition, the celebration was officially dry.
Photograph by Benjamin Gifford; from Oregon Historical Society*

CHAPTER IV
1920-1939

The Failing and Corbett mansions between Fifth and Sixth remained in 1922 as downtown Portland grew around them. The widow Corbett, whose house is in the middle of this picture, provided the city with a tourist attraction by grazing a cow in her side yard. Strangers knocked at the mansions' front doors to ask if they were rooming houses. A butler's stony face was always sufficient answer.

Courtesy of Reed College

In 1919 Portland streetcars carried almost 70 million fares. For mass transit, every year thereafter was downhill. The auto age had taken over.

Cars changed the shape of Portland as radically in the 1920s as streetcars had in the 1890s. The city mushroomed, but not just along tracks. Arterials, streets, trails, and paths—every route stretched for the countryside. By 1925 three quarters of the city lived east of the river. The economy which had once flowed with the river now flowed with gasoline. Factories, warehouses, stores, theaters, parks, and all the fickle servants of rails changed their allegiance to tires.

Union Station became a daily arena for jostling trucks from transfer companies. There were so many, in fact, that some drivers were talking about making trips directly to Seattle or San Francisco by road. What could be easier, especially with the new bridges? No more fighting downtown traffic. One could drive right over the river at Sellwood and Ross Island, and soon would be able to cross at St. Johns, too.

What about the river itself?

By the mid-twenties the Willamette was so polluted there was no more swimming or fishing. Hardly anyone even took excursions by steamer anymore. In fact, the docks were so decayed that the city built a great sea wall along the west bank. The river through downtown became a ditch.

In addition to the car, Portland in the 1920s digested another 50,000 people. The town had grown more rapidly in other decades, but this time seemed different. During this decade Portland crossed some imaginary line between large town and small city. It became more sophisticated and more fragmented; more diverse and more prejudiced; more powerful nationally, yet less dominant in its own region.

At the end of the 1920s Portland's economy seemed healthy as ever. It was not, however, immune to national depression. In the thirties construction and business activity fell first, followed closely by production in timber and agriculture. A Hooverville town of shanties sprung up in Sullivan's Gulch. Thousands of proud workers took public jobs improving roads and parks. There was even union activity and striking, virtually unthinkable before Portland grew from town to city.

By 1939 Portland looked a bit threadbare. A decade of just getting by had taken its toll. Ironically, the river itself was the one bright spot. In 1938 the city of 300,000 decided to stop dumping raw sewage into its prime asset. Voters finally approved construction of the first treatment plant.

Downtown surged with construction during the 1920s. This excavation for the Pacific Building in 1925 cost Mrs. Corbett her grove of trees and cow pasture. The occasion prompted an ambivalent Oregonian *editorial complaining that progress, while* necessary, *meant destroying stately buildings. Mrs. Corbett's house lasted another ten years until it gave way to the present Greyhound Bus Depot.*

From Delano Studio/Acme

Longshoremen in 1922 load cedar logs directly from rail cars onto a ship bound for Japan. Despite new machinery, work on the docks still required mainly muscle and sweat.
From Oregon Historical Society/Dock Commission

Dredging the 108-mile channel from Portland's harbor to the ocean has always received high priority.
Courtesy of City of Portland Archives/Photo-Art

Swan Island prior to development had the ship channel on the east—to the right in this photo.

From Delano Studio/Brubaker

By 1928 the Corps of Engineers had dredged a new channel and virtually made a new Swan Island—the channel and island in use today. Portland's first airport was on Swan Island until the current site opened in 1940. Travellers were delighted to have a trans-Cascade air route east via the Columbia Gorge. "Instead of being compelled to surmount high mountains, the eastbound planes have egress through the water-level pass at a low altitude."

From Delano Studio/Brubaker

106

The six-masted schooner
Oregon Pine *loads at the*
Harvey Lumber Company dock
about 1920.

From Oregon
Historical Society

By the mid-1920s the downtown waterfront was a mess. To clear the debris and cure the problem of flooding, the seawall was built in 1928 along the west bank of the Willamette. The wall extends for almost one mile from the foot of Southwest Jefferson to the foot of Northwest Glisan. These two photographs show virtually identical scenes before and after the wall was built.

Photographs from Oregon Historical Society/ City of Portland

As Portland's bridge of entry, St. Johns has always attracted photographers.
From Delano Studio/Angelus

The main span of the St. Johns Bridge is lowered into place in January 1931. This graceful structure, for many years the longest suspension bridge in the country, was formally opened during the 1931 Rose Festival.

From Oregon Historical Society

Between 1925 and 1927 the Ross Island and Sellwood Bridges were built and the Burnside Bridge was replaced. Here people await the parade at the west end of the new Burnside Bridge in May 1926. The march will pass Hirsch-Weis, forerunner of today's White Stag Company.
Photograph by Arthur Prentiss; from Oregon Historical Society

By 1926 there was regular bus service to other major cities as well as such recreation areas as the Pacific coast. Larger buses included separate areas for women and smokers.
From Oregon Historical Society

With its railroad-like grill, a Union Pacific Stages bus enters the stage depot on Southwest Park and Yamhill in 1933. The bus terminal moved to its present location on Southwest Fifth and Taylor in 1939.

Courtesy of City of Portland Archives

The Meier and Frank Company posted play-by-play information for the 1932 World Series across from the Pioneer Courthouse lawn. The cast iron streetlight standards were a downtown hallmark even then. To preserve continuity with the past, the city continues to cast and install standards of this design.

From Oregon Historical Society/Oregon Journal

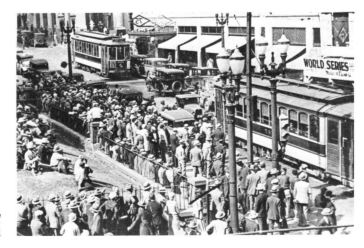

From Oregon Historical Society/Oregon Journal

The good life in Oregon's great out-of-doors.
From Delano Studio/Acme

The twenty-five-acre Municipal Auto Camp on North Union was Portland's first. Camping cost a quarter per car in 1922. "Deluxe cottages" were also available. Auto camps gradually evolved into motels.

From Oregon Historical Society/Oregonian

From December 1936 through June 1949 Portland was one of the few American cities to require motor vehicle inspection. This station was at the corner of Southeast Powell and Milwaukie. Inspectors checked thirteen safety items such as lights and brakes.

From Oregon Historical Society

Portland's early motorists had all the modern conveniences. In 1926 the Campbell Towing Company operated from 450 Southwest Stark.

From Delano Studio

*Horsedrawn wagons such as
this at the corner of Southeast
Seventeenth and Clay remained
a common scene even as cars
and trucks invaded
neighborhoods.*
*From Oregon Historical
Society/City of Portland*

Delano Studio/Acme

THE INTERNATIONAL CROSSROADS, E. 82ᴰ AND SANDY.

Looking north in 1926 toward today's International Airport. Photograph by Roy Norr; from Oregon Historical Society

The automobile helped transform the neighborhood market into the supermarket. This 1930s Pay n 'Takit grocery was part of the early Safeway chain.

Photograph by Arthur Prentiss; from Oregon Historical Society

The Jesus sign has been a landmark since being placed on the roof of the old Apostolic Faith Mission at Front and Burnside in 1918. The sign was transferred to the new building at Sixth and Burnside in 1922. Built entirely with volunteer labor, the structure remains imposing even without the twenty feet lost in the widening of Burnside in the 1920s.
Courtesy of Apostolic Faith Church

The 1927 plan for developing the Servite Fathers' Sanctuary of Our Sorrowful Mother on Northeast Sandy was even grander than the fifty-eight-acre setting of chapels, grottoes, gardens, and statuary which actually resulted;
From Delano Studio

This 1938 crowd heard mass before the altar at the Sanctuary of Our Sorrowful Mother. The altar is hewn from granite at the base of a cliff. A bronze statue of Mary was installed atop the cliff in 1933.
From Oregon Historical Society/Oregon Journal

The University of Oregon Medical School began in 1887 in a vacant grocery store behind its sponsor, Good Samaritan Hospital. This is its second home, built in 1892 at Twenty-Third and Lovejoy.
Courtesy of University of Oregon Health Sciences Center

On June 28, 1931, Fred Meyer, a grocer, opened his Hollywood Public Market at Northeast Sandy and Forty-First. Chain stores such as this along major arterials spelled the decline of many small, neighborhood retailers.
From Oregon Historical Society/Oregonian

Despite availability of heavy machinery, hand labor built most of the Balch Creek Sewer Project in 1921. A survey in 1929 ranked Portland's public facilities fourth among the nation's twenty-five largest cities. Its sewer system, however, was graded "below average." Not surprising! Until 1938, the city of over 300,000 people dumped all its sewage raw into the Willamette.
From Oregon Historical Society

*In the summer of 1924 fishing
in Laurelhurst Lake offered an
attractive alternative to the
polluted Willamette.*
*Courtesy of Portland Parks
and Recreation Bureau*

By 1920 Reed College already enjoyed a national reputation for quality and innovation. Perhaps the college's conservative neighbors were reassured about the normality of its students when freshmen engaged in their annual lakeside battle with sophomores.

From Oregon Historical Society/Oregon Journal

The products of a public school industrial arts class show a growing interest in water as a source of recreation.

Courtesy of Portland Public Schools

In 1910 the Zehntbauer brothers and Carl Jantzen started their Portland Knitting Company, a retail store at Second and Alder. Jantzen designed a rib-stitch swim suit for members of the Portland Rowing Club and the company gradually turned to manufacturing. All three partners agreed Jantzen suits would sell better than Zehntbauer suits, so adopted Jantzen as the company name in 1918.

Courtesy of Jantzen Incorporated

The Columbia upstream from the mouth of the Willamette remained attractive for swimming. This early twenties beach on the south shore of Hayden Island was close to the later development of Jantzen Beach Amusement Park and today's Jantzen Beach Mall.

Photograph by Arthur Prentiss; from Oregon Historical Society

By the time of this 1931 photo the Western Union bicycles had been a familiar sight for four decades. Telegram deliveries peaked during the Second World War, when Western Union had almost 100 full-time delivery people, half of whom operated by bicycle. The familiar spit-and-polish uniforms were a casualty of the war due to shortage of materials.

From Delano Studio/Acme

For four decades Portlanders enjoyed the Jantzen Beach Amusement Park on Hayden Island. The south end of the east promenade, shown here in the 1920s, included the dance hall, Ferris wheel, and Red Bug.

Courtesy of Jantzen Beach Center

Big bands brought big crowds to the Jantzen Beach ballroom in the 1930s. A large shopping center, convention facilities, and residential units began to replace the amusement park during the 1960s.

Courtesy of Jantzen Beach Center

The talkies took over Broadway's Music Box Theatre in 1929. It closed as Liberty Theatre in 1959. Portland was famous in theatre circles for its ornate signs hung horizontally over the streets.
From Delano Studio/Acme

During the 1920s newspapers competed strongly with each other. The Oregon Journal, *its presses and mailroom shown here, faced* The Oregonian, The Portland Daily News, *and* The Portland Telegraph.

From Oregon Historical Society

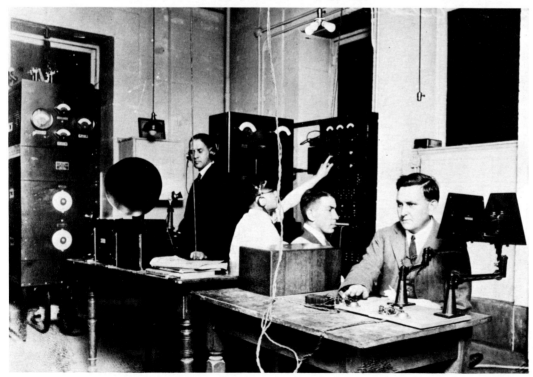

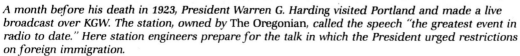

A month before his death in 1923, President Warren G. Harding visited Portland and made a live broadcast over KGW. The station, owned by The Oregonian, *called the speech "the greatest event in radio to date." Here station engineers prepare for the talk in which the President urged restrictions on foreign immigration.*

From Oregon Historical Society/Oregonian

From town crier to cable
television, urban life features
people who specialize in
information. In 1921 the Crane
Letter Company in the 200
block of Morrison used
nothing but the latest in
copying machines.
From Delano Studio/Acme

The Hollywood Theatre on Sandy near Forty-First was one of the city's first opulent "movie palaces." Lounges often included grand pianos.
From Delano Studio/Acme

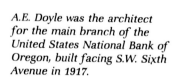

A.E. Doyle was the architect for the main branch of the United States National Bank of Oregon, built facing S.W. Sixth Avenue in 1917.

From Oregon Historical Society

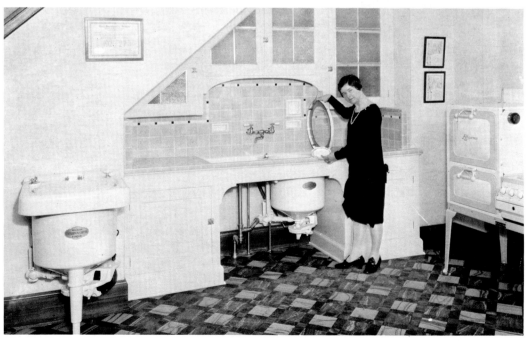

This demonstration kitchen from the late 1920s featured an automatic dishwasher.
From Delano Studio/Acme

The Portland Gas and Coke Company delivers its briquets for home heating. Briquets were a byproduct of converting coal to gas.
From Delano Studio

By the 1920s competing power companies were rapidly wiring Portland. A truck from Northwestern Electric Company, later part of Pacific Power and Light Company, unloads new poles for electric lines.
Courtesy of Pacific Power and Light Company/ Angelus

Internal combustion engines improved handling of wood products so important to the city's well being.
From Delano Studio

Eastmoreland in the early 1920s was just beginning to develop.
  From Delano Studio/Brubaker

Unfortunately for the F.E. Taylor Company, Portland's 1930 population was exactly half the 600,000 predicted here. The city had grown by 40,000 during the 1920s, but would gain only 3,000 more during the 1930s.
  From Oregon Historical Society

Portland's Population
600,000 *by* 1930
This corner is in direct line of Development
Take time by the forelock. We can offer you a most attractive proposition

F. E. TAYLOR CO.

INSIDE PROPERTY DEALERS
YEON BLDG.

During the 1920s Portlanders everywhere cultivated roses, shrubs, gardens, and trees. All were proud of the Rose City.

From Oregon Historical Society

The Great White Fleet calls upon Portland in the late 1930s.

Courtesy of Michael and Susan DesCamp

131

Rain has softened the 1938 scene looking west along the streetcar tracks at West Burn- and Twenty-Third.
From Delano Studio/Acme

Miniature golf became a national pastime between the wars. This course, The Tom Thumb, flourished at the corner of Southeast Sixth and Hawthorne. In 1936 greens fees were twenty-five cents.
From Delano Studio/Acme

Swedish Society Linnea traveled on the steamer Swan down the Willamette River for a picnic before most excursion boats stopped operating from Portland late in the 1920s.
Courtesy of Oskar and Mary Nastrom

Even as river excursions declined, trips by rail and auto increased. Here a Union Pacific train brings Portlanders to Multnomah Falls. The Falls area at the time was managed by the city as a park because of its popularity as a destination on the old Columbia River Highway.

Photograph by Arthur Prentiss; courtesy of Portland Parks and Recreation Bureau

The Pacific Coast Rescue and
Protective Service ran the
Portland Commons, a mission-
settlement house in the
Burnside area at 22 Northwest
Front.
From Delano Studio/Acme

Seven thousand people heard the Philharmonic Society concert in Civic Stadium on June 28, 1936. The orchestra began in the early 1890s; the Youth Philharmonic in 1925. Courtesy of Frank M. Womack.

The Rose Festival remained in full swing even through the Depression years. Schools provided the Maypole dancers to the 1930 festival in Civic Stadium.

From Oregon Historical Society/Oregon Journal

Rundown housing somewhere in Portland's southwest during the 1930s came complete with a two-story outhouse. "America's most beautiful gardens" must refer to some other site.

From Oregon Historical Society

Portland between the wars kept its old reputation as a wide-open town. Good citizens usually just winked at bootlegging, gambling, and vice. Occasionally, however, sound politics would require a few raids. These slot machines are the 1939 model.
From Oregon Historical Society/City of Portland

First the city, then the state, and then in greater measure the Federal government operated public works programs for the unemployed during the Depression.
From Oregon Historical Society/Oregon Journal

A small city made from plywood, cardboard, and corrugated iron occupied Sullivan's Gulch from Northeast Twenty-First to Grand Avenue during the 1930s. To feed themselves, many residents scavenged garbage cans throughout Irvington and Laurelhurst. Shacks under the Grand Avenue overpass appeared in June 1941, just before the city razed its only Hooverville.
From Oregon Historical Society/City of Portland

Governor Julius Meier called out the Oregon National Guard to the Multnomah County Armory on Northwest Tenth during the bitter 1934 Longshoremen strike. The guardsmen's weapons remained silent, but four longshoremen were wounded by local police before the strike was over.
     From Oregon Historical Society/Oregon Journal

Southwest Eleventh and Burnside was known as Auto Row.
     Courtesy of City of Portland Archives

Mayor Joseph K. Carson (center) joins in a 1938 demonstration for clean rivers. Shortly thereafter, voters approved the city's first sewage treatment plant.
     From Oregon Historical Society/Photo-Art

Time hung heavy for many during the Depression. At the St. Vincent De Paul library on Southwest Third and Ankeny, twenty-two thousand men had used the reading room by 1937.

From Oregon Historical Society/Angelus

Throughout its history Portland has been a major center for hiring casual and seasonal labor for shipping, logging, agriculture, and mining. Thousands descended on the Burnside area. In the 1920s the Star Employment Agency at 21 Northwest Second ran one of the better-known recruitment centers.

From Oregon Historical Society

An employee of the Jantzen Company, Northeast Twentieth and Sandy Boulevard, draws yarn in 1937. Most of Portland's work forces remained employed during the Depression, although often on reduced hours and usually in constant fear of being laid off.

From Oregon Historical Society/Oregon Journal

A 1930s aerial that could have been made anytime up to 1950. Portland's downtown changed very little during the Depression and war years.
From Delano Studio/Brubaker

Longshoremen in 1937 celebrate the end of their strike at the Bluebell Tavern in Burnside. Portland docks, trucking, and heavy industry were being organized, putting and end to the long non-union era.
From Oregon Historical Society/Oregon Journal

The nation's largest public market bravely announced its opening in December 1933. Boycotted by some former tenants of the Yamhill Public Market and surrounded by litigation and controversy, the market was in economic trouble within two years. The Oregon Journal bought the building in 1946. In 1969 it was razed to make way for park development along the river.
From Oregon Historical Society

4005
Brubaker Aerial Surveys
Portland, Oregon

CHAPTER V
1940-1959

Broadway at night, April 1940.
Photograph by
Alfred A. Monner

In 1880 a prominent Oregon writer urged "that our free-and-easy way of living, doing business and enjoying life should never be exchanged for the straight-laced methods of the older States." The words could have been echoed by most Portlanders during the 1940s. World War II brought major and lasting change.

During the war, heavy industry dominated the economy for the first time. Fully half the work force was involved directly in building ships and heavy machines. Food and timber still meant dollars and jobs, but the thousand-log float was no longer the Willamette's prime symbol.

Heavy industry brought social change, too. Almost 70,000 newcomers showed up to work in factories and shipyards—so many the federal government had to build vast housing projects. The town's Black population tripled, while its citizens of Japanese heritage vanished.

Wartime Portland was crowded, still a bit shabby from the Depression, and straining to meet demands for schools, transportation, and other public services. As a port, the town was also usually crowded with service men and women in search of entertainment and a touch of home.

When the war ended, Portland jumped back into its cars. Within a few years, dozens of nineteenth century cast iron buildings had been torn down to make way for improvements to Harbor Drive. The landmark Portland Hotel yielded to a parking lot, the bus company lost more and more riders, and the Banfield Freeway was opened as the first of the super roads.

Portland was lucky during the fifties. While other cities were losing population, it held its own. Moreover, big money found its way into the city as well as suburbs. Nothing, for example, was more imposing or expensive than Lloyd Center, finally opened in 1960.

Along with the luck there was a touch of smugness. Some older areas, such as South Portland, were written off along with most of the remaining cast iron buildings. Irvington was considered to be "going Black" and dropped from the informal list of good neighborhoods. Plans were laid for great freeways which would flatten houses and make the city little more than a passing blur.

During the fifties the thousands of immigrants to Portland's suburbs brought with them an attitude long familiar to Oregon settlers. They had escaped to Eden. Yet there was a slight variant to the theme within that generation, for it had fled its own concept of Hades: the large city.

Why worry about Portland? There were always more berry fields to convert to houses and malls.

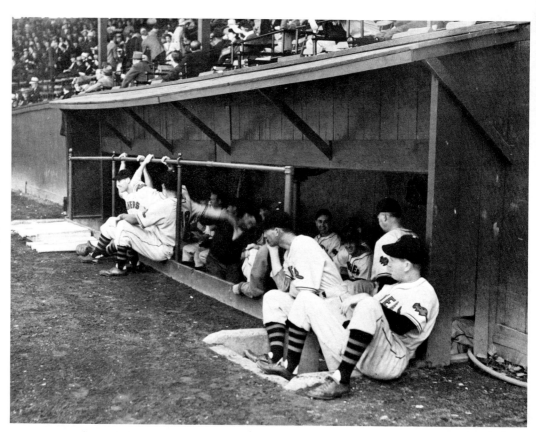

The Portland Beavers were
known as the Lucky Beavers
when they played AAA ball in
Vaughn Street Field from 1903
through 1955. "Lucky" vanished
from the name when they
moved to Civic Stadium
beginning with the 1956 season.
Here in 1941 they were still
very much part of the national
pastime.

Photograph by
Alfred A. Monner

With the spread of downtown
during the 1920s, Chinatown
had moved north of Burnside
along Northwest Fourth. These
announcements of the 1940
Chinese New Year activities
were posted among calls for
Chinese-American citizens to
picket ships loading scrap
metal for Japan.

Photograph by
Alfred A. Monner

In May 1941 the Portland
Beavers opened another
season at Vaughn Street Field.
The stadium existed at the
corner of Vaughn and
Northwest Twenty-Fourth from
1901 until 1955.
*Photograph by
Alfred A. Monner*

Clubs, churches, and stores for
ethnic groups clustered along
Union Avenue in the 1930s and
40s.

*Photograph by
Alfred A. Monner*

Portland readies for a blackout drill just a month before Pearl Harbor.
From Oregon Historical Society/Oregon Journal

From Oregon Historical Society/Photo-Art

In 1942 Japanese-Americans were torn from their West Coast homes, farms, and businesses and interned in camps for the rest of the war. Here soldiers help some of the 3,500 persons forced into temporary quarters at the Portland Assembly Center: converted stables in the Pacific International Livestock building.
From Oregon Historical Society/Oregon Journal

The University of Portland band, speakers, and friends at Union Station send students to war in 1943. In 1901 the Congregation of the Holy Cross bought a struggling Methodist college established the previous decade and called Portland University. A four-year college for men developed in the mid-1920s. The university became fully coeducational in 1951.
Courtesy of University of Portland

The Reverent T. Terakawa and his family of five occupied this apartment equipped only with cots and mattresses and whatever possessions evacuees salvaged from their former homes. One teenager later remembered confusion, fear, and discomfort along with occasional rocks over the fence aimed at those in the Portland Center.
Photograph by Alfred A. Monner

The George A. White Servicemen's Center on Southwest Third near Stark, along with the U.S.O. and the YMCA, helped thousands of servicemen.
Courtesy of Frank M. Womack.

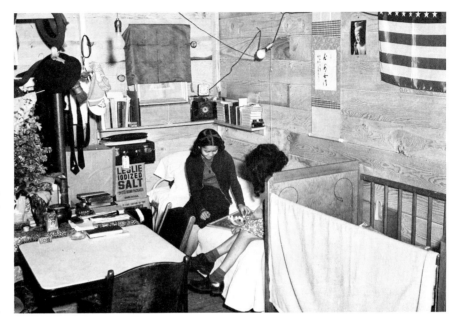

The landfill along the Columbia River provided the site for Portland's new airport, officially opened in 1940.
Photograph by Alfred A. Monner

City and industries operated round the clock. Power from Bonneville Dam, finished in 1937, was a key to the new Northwestern industrial strength. During the war, Vancouver's new Aluminum Company of America plant consumed more electricity than the entire city of Portland.

From Oregon Historical Society

The new Kaiser shipyard launches its first Liberty ship on May 19, 1941. By the end of the war, shipyards in Portland and Vancouver had delivered 756 vessels to the United States and its allies. An additional 500 ships had been outfitted or loaded in Portland.

From Oregon Historical Society

Yards of the Oregon Shipbuilding Company in St. Johns in 1943. At the peak of the war 125,000 people worked in shipbuilding in Portland and Vancouver.

From Oregon Historical Society

Nate Cohn's Stars of Tomorrow talent show continued throughout the war on KGW. The show ran thirty years on radio and another seven on television before ending in the 1960s.
Courtesy of Star Furniture Company

An all-woman cleanup crew for tankers at Commercial Iron Works in Linnton in 1944. Portland yards supposedly had the highest percentage of women working in American shipyards.
From Oregon Historical Society/Photo Art

Courtesy of Jantzen, Inc.

Government contractors built over 17,000 dormitories, barracks, and apartment houses for shipyard workers when the city of 300,000 in 1940 could not house 70,000 newcomers. Huge housing tracts, open to the public in 1944, included Vanport City, Guild's Lake, and St. Johns. These Swan Island workers in 1943 paid $10.15 a week for meals. A million meals monthly were served just at the four housing projects adjacent to Swan Island.

From Oregon Historical Society/Oregon Journal

Vaudeville and burlesque brought crowds to the Nu Gaiety Theatre at First and Main. People had money to spend and the town operated around the clock. The candy counter was a popular arena for Portland's theatre crowd. Photograph by Ralph Vincent; courtesy of Phil Downing Associates

Country music, Oregon style, 1942.
From Delano Studio/Acme

*Two weeks before the war
ended in 1945, Portlanders still
had to contend with rationing
and aging vehicles.*
*Photograph by
Alfred A. Monner*

*The crowd celebrating the end
of the war with Japan is
photographed from* The
Oregon Journal *building
August 15, 1945.*
*From Oregon Historical
Society/Oregon Journal*

TRADE IN OLD EQUIPMENT
Top Allowances NOW during *Sandy's* Dicker Month

FOR NEW MOVIE CAMERAS and EQUIPMENT

KODAKS
CAMERAS
MOVIES
PAY
NOTHING
DOWN

A war surplus jeep serves as grandstand while Washington beats Lincoln in a high school baseball game at Kamm Field on Southwest Salmon and Sixteenth in April 1949.
From Oregon HIstorical Society/Oregon Journal

Once rationing ended and consumer production restarted, Portland joined in the buying spree. Sandy's Camera Shop accepted old cameras as trade-ins on postwar equipment. In 1945 the Southwest Alder shop had been in business for three decades.

Courtesy of Sandy's Camera Shops

157

Rose Festival time always included a visit to Lambert Gardens near Reed College. The Royal Rosarians, established in 1912, were part of this 1947 ceremony to preserve the Queen's footprint.
Photograph by Alfred A. Monner

The 1947 Rose Parade ran from Holladay Park past Sears onto Grand Avenue. Sullivan's Gulch, at the lower right, now holds the Banfield Freeway.
From Oregon Historical Society/Oregonian

Young people from Portland's east side began holding a Junior Rose Festival in 1918. The Junior parade, now the largest of its type in the United States, became part of the Senior Festival in 1936. Here the Junior Rose Court visits Jantzen Beach in 1949.
Photograph by Hugh Ackroyd; courtesy of Jantzen Beach Center

The 1946 Rose Court welcomes the fleet—or vice versa. Navy ships became a regular part of Rose Festival activities beginning in 1953.
Photograph by Gladys Gilbert; courtesy of Portland Rose Festival Association

As skiing grew popular, a ski jump contest was included in Rose Festival events during the 1950s. Skiers preview the jump specially built in Multnomah Stadium for the 1953 festival.
Photograph by Alfred A. Monner

In 1946 the Alpenrose Dairy on Southwest Shattuck Road enjoyed a rural setting. By the 1960s, the dairy had added its popular Western street, bicycle tracks, Little League stadium, and tour facilities.
From Delano Studio/Brubaker

Vanport City was built on a landfill now the site of Delta Park. By the end of World War II, about 19,000 people lived in its 5,300 houses, trailers, and barracks.

From Oregon Historical Society

The Vanport basketball team in 1946 reflects the area's multiracial population. Portland's small prewar Black community tripled during the war as a result of recruitment by war industries. Before the war—and after the Vanport flood—until the 1960s, Blacks were segregated into housing in Albina and adjacent neighborhoods.

From Delano Studio/Acme

Vanport residents—lucky to escape with their lives—were put up in barracks and condemned trailers on Swan Island and other sites all over town.

From Oregon Historical
Society/Oregonian

Because of extraordinarily heavy spring runoffs, Vanport was fifteen feet below Columbia River water level by the end of May 1948. On Memorial Day the dike broke. A wall of water wiped out the town, leaving almost 20,000 without homes and an estimated fifteen people dead.
From Oregon Historical Society

Multnomah County Sheriff's Deputies were among the thousands inoculated against typhoid after the flooding. The Sheriff's Department was one of the few public agencies to deal with the flood without criticism.
Courtesy of Multnomah County Division of Public Safety

164

Flood victims, angry at rising rents and charging lack of help from public housing authorities, demonstrated in front of City Hall on June 20, 1948.

From Oregon Historical Society/Oregon Journal

In 1952 the coffee shop of Portland State Extension Center still reflected the heavily male and veteran enrollment. Opened in 1948 as Vanport Extension Center, it moved following the flood to the Oregon Shipyard in St. Johns. In 1952 it occupied the old Lincoln High School, now Lincoln Hall. It became a four-year college in 1955 and Portland State University in 1969.

Courtesy of Portland State University Archives

The same high water which destroyed Vanport inundated Portland's east side and closed the Morrision Street Bridge for a month. Two weeks after the Vanport disaster, water still reached to Southeast Third Avenue.

From Oregon Historical Society

The Portland Art Museum was the Northwest's first public museum when it opened in 1905. Its current building, built in the 1930s, earned Portland architect Pietro Belluschi international acclaim. This sculpturing class in the early 1950s reflects the museum's traditional commitment to education.

Photograph by
Alfred A. Monner

Southwest Montgomery Drive
on January 19, 1950, during
another one of those Silver
Thaws.

Photograph by
Alfred A. Monner

Teenagers in Portland of the
'50s met at drive-ins after
cruising Broadway on a Friday
or Saturday night. The Tic-Toc
was a landmark at the
junction of East Burnside and
Sandy Boulevard.

From Oregon
Historical Society

TIK TOK

TIME TO EAT

The Korean War meant callups once more. In September 1950 184 draftees on their way to Fort Ord, California, line up outside the army recruiting station on Southwest Taylor between Fourth and Fifth.
      From Oregon Historical Society/Oregon Journal

After a wartime truce, unionization drives and strikes resumed. This 1950 hotel striker shares the sidewalk with a counter-picket.
      From Oregon Historical Society/Oregon Journal

Mr. and Mrs. C.T. Higgins in January 1951 beside the atomic bomb shelter they built in their backyard on Southeast Sherrett.
    From Oregon Historical Society/Oregon Journal

Comparing the catch on the beach at Sauvie Island in 1953. This scene at "Social Security Beach" has been familiar to Portlanders for over a century. Photograph by Alfred A. Monner

Waiting for the evening trolley at Sandy and Burnside looking east from Twelfth in 1948.
Courtesy of City of Portland Archives

During the 1950s the 2400 block of Southwest First was in the heart of the South Portland neighborhood business district. The closeknit community of Jews and Italians was, however, already in decline. Urban renewal was not far behind.

Photograph by Gerald H. Robinson

Many of Portland's streetcars made their last runs in February of 1950. Three years later cars were burned in a Willamette River swamp to retrieve their scrap metal.
From Oregon Historical Society/Oregon Journal

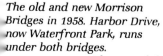

The old and new Morrison Bridges in 1958. Harbor Drive, now Waterfront Park, runs under both bridges.
Photograph by Alfred A. Monner

CHAPTER VI
1960-1979

Portland Trail Blazers win the 1977 National Basketball Association championship. The following day an estimated quarter of a million people gathered downtown for a spontaneous parade.
Photograph by Ralph Perry; courtesy of Portland Trail Blazers

In the mid-1970s several surveys ranked Portland among the nation's most livable large cities. Based upon criteria ranging from clean government to clean rivers, the ranking only confirmed what natives already knew: Portland was number one. People and nature had worked together for the honor: beauty lay in both roads and rivers, energy in both economy and water, friendliness in both climate and people.

Portlanders were proud of their city, and with justice. Downtown they had rediscovered the Willamette by converting Harbor Drive to Waterfront Park. Public money had renewed South Portland and built a transit mall, coliseum, community colleges, and freeway system. Private money had done its share with a convention-class hotel, half a dozen glittering bank and office buildings, and hundreds of smaller projects.

Renewal had a more honest meaning for Portland than for many eastern cities. Most of the past lay within memory of a generation or two. The restaurants and shops infiltrating the Burnside area deliberately took on the quaint looks of yesteryear. Old and new blended in the atmospheres of commercial centers such as the Galleria, Johns Landing, and Ports-of-Call—all designed on a small scale as part of an urban rather than suburban landscape.

And the river! Salmon swam again in the shadow of downtown, boaters paddled again to Ross Island, and swimmers frolicked under the St. Johns Bridge.

While there was cause for pride, there were also grounds for modesty. Since the late 1950s, most of the area's people no longer lived in the city. By 1975 Portland held only a third of the population in the four-county region which had doubled in the last fifteen years.

Transportation, as always, was the key to growth. By the early 1970s there were freeways in all four directions from downtown. A huge ellipse linked the four so traffic could cross the city without pause. Portland no longer dominated.

Perhaps the dose of modesty was good for civic smugness. Many Portlanders found a new appreciation for the people-scale of their town. Neighborhoods such as Sellwood, Lair Hill, and Buckman awakened to their surroundings. Structures which once would have been discarded were now refurbished. Organizations flourished in their zeal to advocate conservation and preservation.

Advocacy was a national trend, and Portland could not escape its frequent harshness. Issues involving land use planning, school desegregation, and freeway construction all proved highly controversial. Yet Portland avoided the confrontations common elsewhere. Non-partisan government, while hardly placid, continued its roots in trust and consensus.

If Portland remained small town in how it was governed, it hit the big time in how it was entertained. The Oregon Symphony, Chamber Music Northwest, Double Tee Promotions, Celebrity Attractions, Trail Blazers, and Timbers all helped Portlanders redefine what the best could be.

Portland at the end of the seventies was not the Biggest, not the Richest, and not the Oldest: just the Best.

The South Auditorium urban renewal area relocated some 1,500 people, 200 businesses, and 400 structures for the development of Portland Center. By the time of this picture in June 1963 the clearing had gone as far north as Market and west as Third.
From Oregon Historical Society/City of Portland

Like all cities, Portland has built up and torn down only to build again. These aging houses on Broadway near Clay were slated for demolition in 1962. Already the previous decade of destruction had taken the Portland Hotel and dozens of fine downtown cast iron buildings.
Photograph by Alfred A. Monner

Giant winds from the Columbus Day storm felled trees onto this house at Northeast Williams and Page.
Photograph by Alfred A. Monner

A hurricane raged through the Willamette Valley on October 12, 1962. This damage was outside the St. James Lutheran Church at the corner of Southwest Park and Jefferson.
Photograph by Alfred A. Monner

During the 1960s and early '70s Portland was alive with groups advocating change. Soon after sit-ins began in the deep South, students in a civil rights march pass in May 1960 beside Lincoln's statue in the South Park Blocks.

From Oregon Historical Society/Oregon Journal

The two-year-old River Queen restaurant, once a ferry, is about to be torn from its moorage by the flooding Willamette River on December 24, 1964. The flood spread into the east side and spilled slightly over the west side seawall.

Photograph by Alfred A. Monner

Thousands joined the Peace March in 1969 at Southwest Sixth and Jefferson. After violent events at Kent State University, Portland State University in May 1970 was the scene of student confrontations with police in the South Park Blocks.

From Oregon Historical Society

*As Portland became in the late
1960s more conscious of
enviromental issues and the
effects of demonstrations,
everyone got into the act.*
*Photograph by
Alfred A. Monner*

The annual Bloody Thursday March of the International Longshoremen and Warehousemen's Union honors four San Francisco longshoremen killed during the 1934 waterfront strike.

From Oregon Historical Society

A 1978 Equal Rights demonstration in Waterfront Park shares space with counter-demonstrators.
Photograph by Kathleen Ryan

ELANO STUDIOS©

Sullivan's Gulch in the 1950s shows the first phase of Banfield Freeway construction. The large open space north of the Bonneville Power Administration building was land already cleared for the giant Lloyd Center.
From Delano Studio

Lloyd Center in the early 1970s had proven itself as the largest and one of the most successful shopping malls in the nation. The fifty-six-block commercial, professional, and hotel complex was opened in 1960.
Courtesy of Portland Convention and Visitors Association

The first mall in the nation designed specifically for mass transit opened in May 1978 on twenty-two blocks of Portland's two busiest downtown streets. Tri-Met buses serve the three-county area and in 1979 carried 35 million fares—half as many as streetcars carried sixty years before.
Photograph by Kathleen Ryan

The world has forty-one Benson fountains—forty in Portland and one in Sapporo, Japan. Simon Benson gave the first twenty in 1912 and 1913. Two more, including the one for Portland's sister city, were cast in 1965. In 1974 students at Benson high school, using scrap brass and the original patterns, made four more. The final fifteen were cast in the mid-1970s for the new transit mall.
Photograph by Kathleen Ryan

During the 1960s Portlanders began to put old buildings to new uses rather than tear them down. The open interior of the Olds, Wortman, and King store, shown here about 1910, offered one such opportunity. Developers in the 1970s turned the building at Southwest Tenth and Morrison into the Galleria collection of restaurants and specialty shops.

Store interior from Oregon Historical Society Galleria photograph by Barbara Gundle; courtesy of Willamette Week

The First National Bank tower completed in 1972 at forty stories is the tallest of many new structures which changed the downtown skyline during the seventies. Construction crews seemed to have every corner fenced off, especially south of Jefferson.

Photograph by Barbara Gundle; courtesy of Willamette Week

The world has forty-one Benson foundations—forty in Portland and one in Sapporo, Japan. Simon Benson gave the first twenty in 1912 and 1913. Two more, including the one for Portland's sister city, were cast in 1965. In 1974 students at Benson high school, using scrap brass and the original patterns, made four more. The final fifteen were cast in the mid-1970s for the new transit mall.

Photograph by Kathleen Ryan

By the mid-1970s the South Park Blocks doubled as campus for Portland State University.
Photograph by Kathleen Ryan

In 1961 the Adult and Vocational Education Department of Portland School District #1 received a charter as Portland Community College. PCC opened its new campus on Mt. Sylvania in 1968 with these students among the first to register for classes.
From Oregon Historical Society/Oregon Journal

The Aubrey Watzek Library at Lewis and Clark College opened in 1967.
Photograph by Hugh Stratford; courtesy of Lewis and Clark College

Lewis and Clark College was known as Albany College when it moved in 1942 to the former M. Lloyd Frank estate on Palatine Hill. The estate gardens have been adapted to the east lawn of the college and still offer this magnificent view of Mount Hood.
Courtesy of Lewis and Clark College/Photo Art

*Portland Timbers' Clyde Best
in action in Civic Stadium
against the San Diego Sockers
in 1978. The Timbers' soccer
franchise came to Portland in
1975.*

*Photograph© by
Steven N. Brenner*

Portland began its love affair with the Trail Blazers during their first season in 1970-71. Bill Walton was a key factor in the 1977 NBA Championship.

Photograph by Jay McCalonen;

The winner of the 1961 Oregon Derby at Portland Meadows. Next to Delta Park in North Portland, the track opened in 1946 and rebuilt its grandstand after a 1971 fire. Earlier in the century, several racetracks had been located along trolley lines in what are now residential neighborhoods.
Photograph by

Alfred A. Monner

Portland is proud of its 7,500 acres of park land in 160 locations. The sites include Forest Park, at 5,000 acres the largest wilderness within an American city. The Wildwood Trail through Forest and other West Side parks begins just behind the Western Forestry Center.

Photograph by Mark Beach

Logs were once placed between high wheels and pulled by teams of horses or oxen. This set is displayed outside the Western Forestry Center built in 1971 to replace the Forestry Museum burned in 1964.

Photograph by Mark Beach

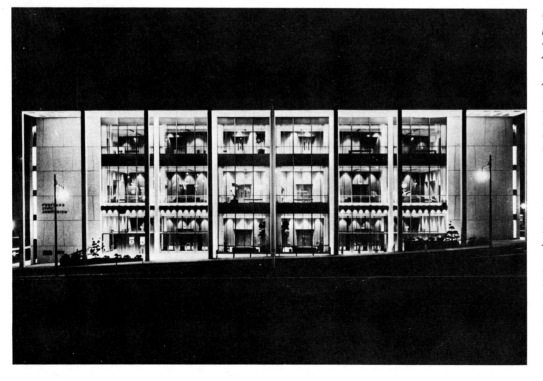

Originally built in 1917 with a portable public dance floor and public baths, the Civic Auditorium was completely remodeled in the early 1960s. A market square in 1852 and the site of the Mechanics Fair Pavilion in the 1870s, this block has been a major place of entertainment for more than a century.

Courtesy of Portland Civic Auditorium

KGW-TV crews record the opening day of Forecourt Fountain in front of Civic Auditorium in 1970. Now called Ira Keller Fountain after a past chairman of the Portland Development Commission, its award-winning design has influenced the architecture of urban parks all over the country.

Courtesy of Bureau of Water Works, City of Portland

Chamber Music Northwest
began its summer festival in
1971 under the sponsorship of
Portland State University. The
series now meets in the
Commons at Reed College,
shown here.
     Photograph by Dan Carter;
     courtesy of Chamber
     Music Northwest

The Oregon Symphony plays a
Sunday family concert about
1976 in Portland Civic
Auditorium.
     Photograph by Stanley B.
     Nagel; courtesy of
     Oregon Symphony Association

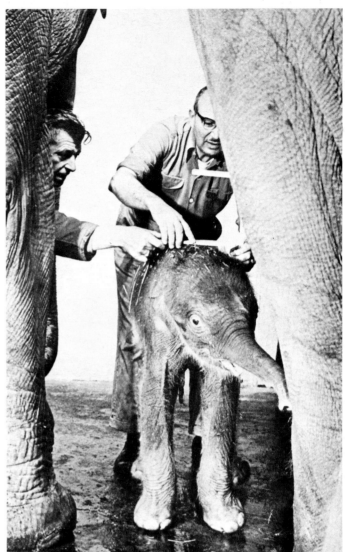

The Oregon Museum of Science and Industry began as a small public museum in 1906. A major fund drive led to construction of its current building in 1957. These 1968 visitors illustrate the attention OMSI gives to enjoyable instruction in the sciences.
Photograph by Alfred A. Monner

Pendleton Woolen Mills is the country's only totally integrated operation from sheep shearing through retail products. These employees work at the Columbia Wool Scouring Mill in the 1970s. The mill began in 1923 and is still located on North Columbia Boulevard.
Courtesy of Pendleton Woolen Mills/Photo Art

196

The Washington Park Zoo next to the Forestry Center and OMSI has been unusually successful in breeding elephants. Packy, shown here in 1960, was the first elephant born in the United States since 1918.

Photograph by David Falconer; from Washington Park Zoo

BEAR DENS. CITY PARK, PORTLAND, OREGON.

From 1925 through 1959 the zoo was part of Washington Park. The area became today's Japanese Garden, the bear pit today's Strolling Pond garden.

From Oregon Historical Society

The Japanese Garden in Washington Park, opened in 1964, reflects Portland's ties to the Orient. The area includes this Strolling Pond garden lined with iris and soothed by a waterfall from the hillside—formerly the bear pit.

Photograph by Mark Beach

Thousands of Portlanders enjoyed People's Day on the Fremont Bridge in November 1973 before traffic was allowed to flow.

From Oregon Historical Society

Portland's newest bridge, the Fremont, was finished in 1973 when the 6,000-ton center span was lifted 170 feet from river level and placed into position. The event, which took only a few hours, attracted engineers from all over the world to join Portlanders on the specially built grandstand. The port remained open to traffic during the entire time of construction.

Photograph by Hugh Ackroyd

Since 1968 KBOO has survived as a listener-supported community radio station. Portland City Councilperson Mildred Schwab, in earphones, joins station volunteers for a publicity photo in 1976 outside the former headquarters on Southeast Belmont. The station now reaches 45,000 listeners from its downtown headquarters on Southwest Yamhill.

Courtesy of KBOO

The Swedish Society Linnea celebrates the annual Festival of Lights in its hall on Northwest Irving. The hall was built in 1909 and is one of the few remaining frame halls in the city. It now houses apartments and offices.
Photograph by Nels Enderberg

The Leikarringen dance team from Sons of Norway Greig Lodge No. 15 performs a traditional weave dance at Central Lutheran Church in 1974. Based in Norse Hall on Northeast Eleventh near Burnside, this team began dancing when its members were children.
Photograph by Glenn Nordby, Jr.

In a scene common since the 1960s, bicycle riders and skate boarders populate the neighborhoods. These were at Southwest Patton and Vista in April 1965.
Courtesy of City of Portland Archives

Neighborhood and ethnic organizations, both revitalized during the 1970s, draw over 300,000 to Waterfront Park each July for Neighbor Fair. KGW-TV, KINK, and KGW radio stations have sponsored the event since 1976.
Photograph by Noreen Brownlie

And still there were Silver Thaws—this one in January 1979.
Photograph by Sue Ford; from Washington Park Zoo.

The Miss Tan Portland won first prize in the 1969 Rose Festival Parade for non-commercial entries. The nationwide pageant has been sponsored in Portland since 1964.
From Oregon Historical Society

The Cascade Runoff, a fifteen-kilometer race from downtown up the Terwilliger Hill and back down Barbur to Waterfront Park, has established itself as a national running event since it began in 1977.
Photograph by Mark Beach

Cinnamon Bear, sponsored by Lipman's Department Store (now Frederick and Nelson's), visits Buckman School in December 1965. The friendly bear and companion to Santa has been a Portland tradition since its origins on KEX radio in 1937.
From Oregon Historical Society/Oregon Journal

The largest floating dry dock on the west coast barely squeezed by the railroad bridge en route to the tip of Swan Island in September 1978. Built in Japan for the Port of Portland, the 982-foot structure will handle even the largest tanker in the Alaska fleet.

Photograph by Ancil Nance; courtesy of Port of Portland

Terminal Four berths the first general cargo ship from the People's Republic of China to call in the United States. Portland II, built in 1946, is the only sternwheeler tug operating in the world. Portland pilots like sternwheelers for practical as well as sentimental reasons: they are highly maneuverable and have equal power in reverse and forward.

Photograph by Jim Douglas; courtesy of Port of Portland

201

Scenes such as this in March 1980 preceded the violent eruption of Mount St. Helens on May 18th. The peak in Washington, only forty-five miles from Portland, continued its historic role as a source of beauty and power.

Photograph by Tim Jewett

The heavy concentration of new buildings south of Jefferson in 1980 gives Portland a new skyline next to the old.

Photo by Kathleen Ryan

Bibliography

Whether you want a general introduction or detailed knowledge, there are fine sources of information about Portland. Here are some ways to get started.

- Work with the staff and in the catalogs at Oregon Historical Society and Multnomah County Library.

- Read *Portland: A Historical Sketch and Guide*, by Terence O'Donnell and Thomas Vaughan.

- Read the two books by E. Kimbark MacColl: *The Shaping of a City* and *The Growth of a City* — and consult the extensive references found in each.

- Consult these three fine special bibliographies:

    1. Kathay Duff, "A Portland Bibliography." In *Time-image*, Volume One, No. 2, June 1979, pages 40–52.

    2. Steve Johnson, "History Resources." In *The Portland Book*, Center for Urban Education, 1979, pages 67–74.

    3. Anthony White's series of seven bibliographies done in 1976 as numbers 1004 through 1010 in the series of urban bibliographies published by the Council of Planning Libraries.

All these materials are available in local libraries.

Index

Acknowledgments

A number of people generously shared with us their extensive knowledge of Portland. We especially want to thank Dr. E. Kimbark MacColl and the following staff of the Oregon Historical Society: Susan Seyl, Elizabeth Winroth, Paul Ewing, Arthur Spencer, and Terence O'Donnell.

While dozens of Portlanders opened their photo collections for us to examine, four were particularly helpful: John (Woody) Conley, Emily Delano, Leonard Delano, and Alfred A. Monner.

Looking back, it seems there were countless places at which one of us looked at pictures. In every case, it meant someone had to find us a place to work and explain the meaning of many images. We deeply appreciate the time, information and willingness to share photographs from Hugh Ackroyd; Alpenrose Dairy; Apostolic Faith Church; Audubon Society of Portland; Shana Beach; Bingham-Willamette Industries; Steve Brenner; Thelma Brown; Noreen Brownlie; Chamber Music Northwest; City of Portland Archives; City of Portland: Bureau of Parks and Recreation, Bureau of Water Works, and Columbia Treatment Plant; Tim Collins; Lana Danaher; Mike and Susan DesCamp; Eastmoreland Hospital; Nels Enderberg; Erickson's Cafe and Concert Hall; J.K. Gill Co., Good Samaritan Hospital and Medical Center; Yani Hara; Hippo Hardware; William Hayes; The Portland Hilton; Holladay Park Hospital; Jantzen Beach Center, Jantzen Inc.; Japanese Garden Society; Jefferson High School; Tim Jewett; Jewish Historical Society of Oregon Inc.; KBOO; KGW-TV; KPTV; Lewis and Clark College; Elmer Mencer; Eugene Messer; Multnomah County Division of Public Safety; Oskar and Mary Nastrom; Neighbors of Woodcraft; Glen Nordby, Jr.; Northwest Natural Gas Co.; Oregon Museum of Science and Industry; Oregon Symphony Association; Pacific Power and Light Company; Pendleton Woolen Mills; Phil Downing Associates; Port of Portland; Portland Art Museum; Portland Civic Auditorium; Portland Convention and Visitors Association; Portland Junior Symphony Association; Portland Public Schools; Portland Rose Festival Association; Portland State University Archives; Portland Timbers; Portland Trail Blazers; Reed College; Gerald Robinson; Sandy's Camera Shop; Sheraton Inn, Roger Shiels; Sons of Norway-Grieg Lodge #15; Star Furniture Company; Tri-Met; U.S. National Archives; University of Oregon Health Sciences Center; University of Portland; Leslie Unthank; Vintage Photos/Elaine Gobel; Washington Park Zoo; Western Forestry Center; *Willamette Week;* and Frank M. Womack.